הגדה של פסח

Visions of Freedom

A Collection of
Inspirational Stories & Parables
on the Passover Haggadah

With New Translation and
Presentation of Laws & Customs

RABBI YOSEF WEISS

C.I.S. PUBLISHERS
New York • London • Jerusalem

כל דכפין
The Year

R' Chaim

R' Chaim is Torah personified. An immense Talmid Chochom who studies at one of the important Kolels in Jerusalem. Going to learn without eating first throws his learning off kilter completely. It's hard to concentrate and his grasp of the issues less firm. Learning Torah was never a "get rich quick" scheme, but food, says the Mishna, is a prerequisite.

It is here, in Linas HaCheses soup kitchen, that R' Chaim finds his breakfast. The fuel that will drive his unrelenting drive to learn Torah for hours on end.

That Torah belong to you, for you were a "feeder of the hungry"

R' Chizkiya

A father of seven who lives on the Dwelling of the Bucharians in Jerusalem. A few weeks ago he lost his job. R' Cheskiya has many things to worry about: Water and electric bills… mortgage… the one thing he doesn't need to worry about, thank G-G, is food. Linas HaChesed takes care of that. Every day he comes in, picks up hot delicious food, all wrapped up, for everyone in the family and goes home. Once there, R' Cheskiya his wife and seven children sit and eat. No food worries.

That peace of mind belong to you, for you were a "feeder of the hungry"

‫ייתי ויאכול‬
Throughout

Rivka

A mother of ten Rivka lives and works in at local store. The wages, unfortunately, are far from enough to pay rent and a few of the bills. In her house the children are hungry. The refrigerator is, literally empty.

Every evening the children come to the obvious place: the warm, welcoming home of Linas HaChesed soup kitchen. When they are done eating they pack up a meal for their mom so that she too, may eat with dignity. Many times she cries when she eats. No those are not tears of sorrow, but those of gratitude and relief. Better days are surly ahead all of them. But for now, another day has passed and everyone is fed. Thank G-D.

Those tears belong to you, for you were a "feeder of the hungry"

Moishele

A ten-year old child from a home of many children that lost their mother. Moishele is learning Torah most of the day, only to return home hungry. He's yet to have eaten a meal. But Moishele knows exactly where one goes when one is hungry: the Linas HaChesed soup kitchen. There's much to think about – he comes in he eats and his hunger is gone…

Moishele returns home, stretches out on this little bed, says Krias Shma and falls peacefully asleep.

That sleep belongs to you, for you were a "feeder of the hungry"

comfortably in a clean and pleasant environment. Visitors to Linas Hachessed can serve themselves from the tasty, attractively arranged food - free to eat to their satisfaction, as Reb Chaim Cohen does not know when they last ate or when they will next have a good meal.

Linas Hachessed is open for three hours every morning and three hours every evening. There is no need to book a place and no one has to give his name. The atmosphere is warm and friendly so that whoever comes to Linas Hachessed feels comfortable, despite the unfortunate circumstances that may have brought them there.

Before Pesach, Reb Chaim introduced a voucher system, distributing vouchers worth NIS 64,000, to be spent at meat, fish and grocery stores, to cover the Yom Tov expenses of families whose circumstances have become known to him through Linas Hachessed, yet who would be ashamed to accept food delivered to them free. Seeing the importance of this form of food distribution, he hopes to continue it during the year as well.

Visitors to Linas Hachessed cannot contain their amazement at this beacon of chessed. Gedolei Yisrael who have witnessed it in action urge all who are able to become partners in this wonderful mitzva, which brings together donors and recipients from all sectors of Klal Yisrael in a spirit of true achdus. Gedolei Yisrael have expressed their view that Linas Hachessed is a great zechus and source of protection for Klal Yisrael, and warm letters of recommendation have been received from distinguished Rabbanim including:

- **Rabbi Steve Amon**
  Cong. Shaare Tefilah Bnei Moshe

- **Rabbi Meyer Bronsdorfer**
  Eideh Hachoredis Jerusalem

- **Rabbi Daniel Frisch** zt"l
  Yeshivas Mekubalim Jerusalim

- **Rabbi Malkiel Kotler**
  Rosh Yeshivas Bais Medrash Govoha Lakewood

- **Rabbi Mattisyohu Salomon**
  Mashgiach Bais Medrash Govoha Lakewood

- **Rabbi Yosef Azran**
  Chef Rabbi Rishon Lazion

- **Rabbi Mordechai Eliyahu**
  Former Chief Rabbi of Israel

- **Rabbi Naftuli Halbershtam**
  Admor of Bobov

- **Rabbi Avigdor Nebinzal**
  Rosh Yeshivah Yeshivath Hakotel

- **Rabbi Moshe Wolfson**
  Yeshiva Torah Vodaath

Jarusalem Open House • לינת החסד
Providing Food for the Poor of Yerushalayim

Number 1 Oneg Shabbos Street in the Meah She'arim district of Yerushalayim looks no different from the other old houses in the neighbourhood; its exterior does not betray the amazing activity going on behind its walls. But this is the headquarters of Linas Hachessed, where approximately 400 portions of food are provided daily to some of Yerushalayim's most destitute residents.

Young and old come to Linas Hachessed. They belong to all sectors of the community: Sefardim and Ashkenazim, chassidim and Litvishe. Some come in every day, whereas others, who had previously been able to provide for themselves and their families comfortably, only come when their poverty and hunger overtakes them and forces them to overcome their pride

Linas Hachessed was founded six years ago by Reb Chaim Cohen of Yerushalayim. He saw that despite the numerous tzedaka and chessed institutions in Yerushalayim, there was still a need for a facility of this kind. The great hardship for many families due to government Social Security cuts and the closure of many kollelim and mosdos in the past three years, has proven how correct his judgement was.

Fathers come in with their children in the morning on a regular basis, so that they shouldn't have to go to cheder on an empty stomach. Avreichim, who are unable to pay their grocery bills and can no longer buy on credit, bring food home for their wives and children. Baalei teshuva, who can no longer eat at their parents homes, widowers and bachelors who have no one to cook for them, and the list goes on .... What they all have in common is that they come to Linas Hachessed for a nourishing meal that they cannot afford to pay for themselves.

Linas Hachessed does not merely sustain these people's hunger; it seeks to provide food whilst retaining their sense of dignity as well. The dining room is a former banquet hall, where everyone can sit

שמואל קמנצקי
Rabbi S. Kamenetsky

2018 Upland Way
Philadelphia, Pa 19131

Home: 215-473-2798
Study: 215-473-1212

בס"ד יום ג' מזמ' אבֿין שרת לפֿזְ

לכבוד הרב הגאון ר' יוסף וונ חיים שליט"א

אחרי דרישת שלום הגדול להדרכה פוב...

קונקורסו של הגאב הכסא הגיון ועמד ...

... בדר' ... מה שאין הדין

... ההאמתה והמדיונות כי. י... הצועל...

... הלומד, לעומים דבר... וזיט... ...

לכבן אמונה וב"פ.

... ... שמחן הדרית שלאת

עמא... ...

דברכה מרובה
[signature]

RABBI ARYEH MALKIEL KOTLER
BETH MEDRASH GOVOHA
LAKEWOOD, N.J. 08701

בעז"ה

ארי' מלכיאל קוטלר
בית מדרש גבוה
לייקוואוד, נ. דז.

יום טבת תשס"ו

בלשון בעל ההגדה כל המרבה לספר ביצי"מ ה"ז משובח כי' ואמרת לבנך
וצ"ע המספר והביאור עלב ה ה' לצאיא. באש ה ובהשפלה בכל דור ודור חיב
אדם לראות עצמו כאילו יצא ממצרים, ובמה פא מ"ל כאילו יצא עצת
ממצרים, וה"ע עד שאמרת להראות פתגו עצ"י בגאולה, והלימוים אצל
תענ ה הך מצלה באמונה ובכל עצ"ים של תירוג, וה'ה הוא יצאו מבשבת

אוחריין וגפלא למעלה עי' י הרבה יום ו"ים עלוצ'ו ה'עוצ בס מריי
סיבונים העולהיבים ליראג ה' שהניה, ולאמפוח שמבות, וזכטן מוסל צוד
מספר על הגאופה אל בסח, להתחיל ה'צ"ן פ כן' להגלף בחוד עצ'ני
עלפוה ואצא מ עפרים על יד' מטלים ופלוחים בגואלא מצ"ים ובפח)
צצירי הפפון לה'ל היבית ליצגת ה' וללימ'וף ה'מאוה ומבוח עובות, כה
יתן ש'אתחפלו בפסיו ואתא לאז'וק, ונה יוס'ל בתביפתו הפביה לה'לב
לצולות טאים ומד וכ'בה לראוה הקיים ה'הגאות כ'ש' צאחק מאעצ'ים
אמ'ינו ופלאות בחפל באמונה

הכוח לכבוד התושה ולעורג
עמה מלכיאל קוטלי

Table of Contents

Introduction

With praise and thanks to the *Ribono Shel Olam*, I take this momentous opportunity to share *Visions of Freedom* with the English-speaking Torah public.

It is on the night of Pesach that *Klal Yisrael* performs the *mitzvah* of reciting the *Haggadah*, together with the festive meal which incorporates the performance of the many *mitzvos* of this special night. The fascinating order and structure; the many intriguing and unusual customs — all these transform the evening into the *seder* night.

In his commentary on the *Haggadah*, the *Sfas Emes* quotes the *Maharal*, who says that the word *seder* alludes to an important concept. Just as there is *seder*, structure, in nature, so too there is a *seder* in miracles and wonders. The *Sfas Emes* points out that the word *seder* alludes to the long *galus* that *Klal Yisrael* suffered in Mitzrayim. That long, bitter exile had not occurred by chance. Rather, each and every step, each and every anguished event, occurred with a *seder* — that is to say, it was intentionally instituted by Hashem, in His mercy, for the sake of His people.

The recital of the *Haggadah* is a major focus of this special night. Yet the array of different subjects that are presented in the *Haggadah* are seemingly unrelated. What, one wonders, is the underlying *seder*, order — the unifying intent of the *Baal Haggadah* when forming this work?

There are differences of opinion as to when the text of the *Haggadah* was instituted. Some say that it was formed by the *Anshei Knesses Hagedolah*, while others, such as the *Avudraham*, attribute it to the times of the *Amoraim*. The portions at the end of the *Haggadah*, which are not found in *Chazal*, are nevertheless attributed to the time of the *Rishonim*. Thus, it is fitting that countless commentaries over the centuries have delved into the hidden treasures that lie within the *Haggadah Shel Pesach*.

With Hashem's help, I have attempted to suggest a theme which offers a clarification for the unique order of the *Haggadah*. In addition, I have presented entertaining parables in the form of short stories, both to establish these unifying points and to offer valuable lessons to the reader.

It is my hope and prayer that this *sefer* will assist us in achieving our ultimate goals in the service of Hashem.

Acknowledgments

First and foremost, I would like to thank **Mrs. P. Soloveitchik** of Yerushalayim, for skillfully editing and perfecting the entire manuscript.

To my sister-in-law, **Perel Davis,** for proofreading the Manuscript and adding her invaluable comments.

A particular note of gratitude to **Mrs. B. Gutman,** for typesetting and handling each request with patience and efficiency.

To **R' Moshe Flohr,** for helping me get over the hurdles.

My thanks to **R' Yitzchok Aryeh Epstein,** for his alacrity and constant encouragement.

I extend my great respect and thanks to **Rabbi Alexander Zissel Ellinson** and his staff at **CIS Publishers,** for their professional presentation of this *sefer.*

I am grateful to **Harav Simcha Schustal,** *shlita, Rosh Yeshivah* of Yeshiva Bais Binyomin of Stamford, CT, **HaRav Shmuel Kamenetsky,** *shlita, Rosh Yeshiva* of the Yeshiva of Philadelphia, and **Harav Aryeh Malkiel Kotler,** *shlita, Rosh Yeshiva* of Beth Medrash Govoha of Lakewood, NJ, for gracing this sefer with their kind words and blessings.

My sincere appreciation to **Rabbi Binyomin Friedland** and **Rabbi Yosef Gelbwachs,** *Roshei Yeshiva* of Mesivta Ohr Chodosh and Bais Medrash Ohr Hatalmud in Lakewood, NJ, where I am fortunate to serve and share in their magnificent work.

Special thanks to my *chaver,* **R' Ephraim Wiederman,** for helping me organize my thoughts.

A note of gratitude to **Rabbi Yedidya Einhorn,** *menahel* of Torah V'yirah D'Satmar of Lakewood, where I am also privileged to serve.

No words suffice to express proper gratitude to my parents, **Mr. and Mrs. Eliezer Weiss;** my dear brother **Reb Shlomo** and his family; and my in-laws, **Rabbi and Mrs. Chaim Yaakov Davis** and family of London, England. May they all be blessed with long life, good health, and enjoy much Torah *nachas* from their families.

To my devoted wife, **Tova,** and all my children, who constantly offer their encouragement and inspiration. May we be worthy to receive Hashem's blessings and continue to grow in His service. May we all merit to greet *Mashiach* speedily, in our days.

Yosef Yona Weiss
Adar 5762 (2002)
Lakewood, NJ

ALSO BY RABBI YOSEF WEISS

In addition to this
Visions of Freedom Haggadah
Rabbi Yosef Weiss is the noted author
of the acclaimed
Visions of Greatness Series.

The ***Visions of Greatness Series***
is an ongoing collection of
Inspirational stories.
Seven volumes in the Series have
already been published.
Volume Eight is being prepared for
publication.

Published and distributed by:
C.I.S. Publishers and Distributors
180 Park Avenue, Lakewood, New Jersey 08701
Tel: (732) 905-3000 Fax: (732) 367-6666

Cover Design: DC Design, Lakewood, New Jersey
Typesetting and Layout: Fit to Print (Bassie Gutman) (732) 367-5273

ISBN 1-56062-334-9 (soft cover)
ISBN 1-56062-335-7 (hard cover)

THE **PRINTH⬡USE**

538 JOHNSON AVENUE
BROOKLYN, NEW YORK 11237
TEL 718.628.6700   718.628.6900 FAX

The Seder   סדר הגדה

Kadesh		קַדֵּשׁ
Urchatz		וּרְחַץ
Karpas		כַּרְפַּס
Yachatz		יַחַץ
Maggid		מַגִּיד
Rachtzah		רָחְצָה
Motzi		מוֹצִיא
Matzah		מַצָּה
Maror		מָרוֹר
Korech		כּוֹרֵךְ
Shulchan Orech		שֻׁלְחָן עוֹרֵךְ
Tzafun		צָפוּן
Barech		בָּרֵךְ
Hallel		הַלֵּל
Nirtzah		נִרְצָה

קַדֵּשׁ

כשחל יו״ט בשבת מתחילין יום הששי.

יאמר בלחש: וַיְהִי עֶרֶב וַיְהִי בֹקֶר,

יוֹם הַשִּׁשִּׁי: וַיְכֻלּוּ הַשָּׁמַיִם וְהָאָרֶץ וְכָל צְבָאָם: וַיְכַל אֱלֹהִים בַּיּוֹם הַשְּׁבִיעִי מְלַאכְתּוֹ אֲשֶׁר עָשָׂה, וַיִּשְׁבֹּת בַּיּוֹם הַשְּׁבִיעִי מִכָּל מְלַאכְתּוֹ אֲשֶׁר עָשָׂה: וַיְבָרֶךְ אֱלֹהִים אֶת יוֹם הַשְּׁבִיעִי וַיְקַדֵּשׁ אֹתוֹ, כִּי בוֹ שָׁבַת מִכָּל מְלַאכְתּוֹ אֲשֶׁר בָּרָא אֱלֹהִים לַעֲשׂוֹת:

כשחל בחול מתחילין כאן

סַבְרִי מָרָנָן וְרַבָּנָן וְרַבּוֹתַי:

בָּרוּךְ אַתָּה יי, אֱלֹהֵינוּ מֶלֶךְ הָעוֹלָם, בּוֹרֵא פְּרִי הַגָּפֶן.

בָּרוּךְ אַתָּה יי, אֱלֹהֵינוּ מֶלֶךְ הָעוֹלָם, אֲשֶׁר בָּחַר בָּנוּ מִכָּל עָם וְרוֹמְמָנוּ מִכָּל לָשׁוֹן וְקִדְּשָׁנוּ בְּמִצְוֹתָיו, וַתִּתֶּן לָנוּ יי אֱלֹהֵינוּ בְּאַהֲבָה (**לשבת:** שַׁבָּתוֹת לִמְנוּחָה וּ)מוֹעֲדִים לְשִׂמְחָה, חַגִּים וּזְמַנִּים לְשָׂשׂוֹן, (אֶת יוֹם הַשַּׁבָּת הַזֶּה וְ)אֶת יוֹם חַג הַמַּצּוֹת הַזֶּה, זְמַן חֵרוּתֵנוּ, (בְּאַהֲבָה) מִקְרָא קֹדֶשׁ, זֵכֶר לִיצִיאַת מִצְרָיִם. כִּי בָנוּ בָחַרְתָּ וְאוֹתָנוּ קִדַּשְׁתָּ מִכָּל הָעַמִּים, (וְשַׁבָּת וּ)מוֹעֲדֵי קָדְשֶׁךָ (בְּאַהֲבָה וּבְרָצוֹן) בְּשִׂמְחָה וּבְשָׂשׂוֹן הִנְחַלְתָּנוּ. בָּרוּךְ אַתָּה יי, מְקַדֵּשׁ (הַשַּׁבָּת וְ)יִשְׂרָאֵל וְהַזְּמַנִּים.

אם חל במוצאי שבת אומרים כאן ברכת בורא מאורי האש וברכת הבדלה
ואח״כ שהחיינו יקנה״ז

בָּרוּךְ אַתָּה יי, אֱלֹהֵינוּ מֶלֶךְ הָעוֹלָם, בּוֹרֵא מְאוֹרֵי הָאֵשׁ:

בָּרוּךְ אַתָּה יי, אֱלֹהֵינוּ מֶלֶךְ הָעוֹלָם, הַמַּבְדִּיל בֵּין קֹדֶשׁ לְחֹל, בֵּין אוֹר לְחֹשֶׁךְ, בֵּין יִשְׂרָאֵל לָעַמִּים, בֵּין יוֹם הַשְּׁבִיעִי לְשֵׁשֶׁת יְמֵי הַמַּעֲשֶׂה. בֵּין קְדֻשַּׁת שַׁבָּת לִקְדֻשַּׁת יוֹם טוֹב הִבְדַּלְתָּ. וְאֶת יוֹם הַשְּׁבִיעִי מִשֵּׁשֶׁת יְמֵי הַמַּעֲשֶׂה קִדַּשְׁתָּ. הִבְדַּלְתָּ וְקִדַּשְׁתָּ אֶת עַמְּךָ יִשְׂרָאֵל בִּקְדֻשָּׁתֶךָ: בָּרוּךְ אַתָּה יי, הַמַּבְדִּיל בֵּין קֹדֶשׁ לְקֹדֶשׁ:

נשים שברכו שהחיינו בהדלקת הנר יזהרו שלא יאמרוהו שנית בשעת קידוש

בָּרוּךְ אַתָּה יי, אֱלֹהֵינוּ מֶלֶךְ הָעוֹלָם, שֶׁהֶחֱיָנוּ וְקִיְּמָנוּ וְהִגִּיעָנוּ לַזְּמַן הַזֶּה:

ושותה בהסבת שמאל דרך חירות ואינו מברך ברכה אחרונה

וּרְחַץ

ואין מברכין על נטילת ידים

כַּרְפַּס

כשמברך יש לכוין לפטור גם את המרור

בָּרוּךְ אַתָּה יי, אֱלֹהֵינוּ מֶלֶךְ הָעוֹלָם, בּוֹרֵא פְּרִי הָאֲדָמָה:

יַחַץ

יקח את המצה האמצעית ויחלקו לשנים וישמור החלק הגדול לאפיקומן

מַגִּיד

יגביה את הקערה עם המצות ויאמר הא לחמא עניא בקול רם

הָא לַחְמָא עַנְיָא דִי אֲכָלוּ אַבְהָתָנָא בְּאַרְעָא דְמִצְרָיִם. כָּל דִּכְפִין יֵיתֵי וְיֵיכוֹל. כָּל דִּצְרִיךְ יֵיתֵי וְיִפְסַח. הָשַׁתָּא הָכָא לְשָׁנָה הַבָּאָה בְּאַרְעָא דְיִשְׂרָאֵל. הָשַׁתָּא עַבְדֵי לְשָׁנָה הַבָּאָה בְּנֵי חוֹרִין.

This is the bread of affliction .... This year we are slaves; next year, may we be free men.

We invite the poor to join us in the Seder with an unflattering description of the meager menu: *"This is the bread of affliction."* Who would be interested in such an invitation?

What is the connection between the two contrasts offered: *This year we are here / slaves; next year, may we be in Eretz Yisrael / free men?*

❀ ❀ ❀

R eb Shimon trudged wearily through the muddy streets of his little village. The sun was sinking rapidly behind the hills. There was no more time to spend chasing down a few more pennies, the *minyan* for *Minchah* would begin in just a few minutes.

He sighed as he reached the *shul* at the end of the street. Here it was, Thursday evening, and he had barely earned enough money to buy a few crusts of bread for the following week. There certainly wasn't enough to buy provisions for Shabbos. Once again, he and his family would have to rely on the generosity of others for the peace and joy of their Shabbos meals.

It is wrong to complain, he told himself sternly. He should be grateful that the people of his village were of such a kind nature. He could not remember the last time he had received less then three or four invitations for each Shabbos. Their generous hosts always made them feel as if Reb Shimon and his family were doing them a favor, instead of the other way around. While they never ate the Shabbos meals in their own home, Reb Shimon's family always enjoyed pleasant, companionable *seudos* in the houses of their hosts.

Still, Reb Shimon had to admit to himself how disturbed he felt by his inability to provide for his own family. It was embarrassing to be

This is the bread of affliction, which our ancestors ate in the land of Egypt. Whoever is hungry, let him come and eat. Whoever is needy, let him come and join in Passover's observance. This year, we are here. Next year, may we be in Eretz Yisrael. This year, we are slaves. Next year, may we be free men.

forced to eat, week after week, in the homes of others. How he wished there was some way he could manage to earn enough money to make Shabbos in the homey comfort of his own house!

Reb Shimon forced himself to put these depressing thoughts out of his mind as *Minchah* began. When the *davening* ended, he made his way out of the *shul* and turned towards the tiny house at the end of the village.

Gittel was waiting for him. She had prepared the usual evening meal: dry bread with a glass of hot tea. They could afford nothing more.

"How did it go today?" she asked hopefully.

"We received an invitation to join Reb Chaim Silver's family for the Shabbos meals," he said quietly. "I thanked Reb Chaim for his generosity, and told him we would come."

Gittel nodded silently. Reb Shimon had given her his answer: Once again, he had not earned enough money to provide them and their four children with food for Shabbos.

For a short time, they ate in silence. Then he looked up. "Gittel, I have made up my mind," he told her. "This is the last time we will eat our Shabbos meals in the homes of others. One way or another, I will earn enough money so that we may eat at home."

Gittel looked at him with surprise. Her husband already labored as a porter from morning until night, doing whatever jobs he could to earn money. How could he possibly find a way to do more than he already did?

However, she did not argue. She understood how it frustrated him to constantly depend on others for their Shabbos *seudos*. "I am sure that with Hashem's help, You will manage," she said encouragingly. "I, too, will do everything I can. Perhaps we can manage to cut a few more corners during the week, in order to have more for Shabbos."

Shabbos passed in its usual pleasant manner. The Silvers were gracious, friendly hosts. Reb Shimon did not mention his new goal again, but Gittel knew that he had not changed his mind. Somehow, their family would find a way to make their own Shabbos.

For the next few days, Reb Shimon did everything he could to earn enough pennies to put food on his Shabbos table. He awakened before dawn and did not return home until long after dark, drained and exhausted from his feverish labors during the day. Still, when Friday arrived, Reb Shimon and Gittel joyously counted the money he had earned during the week. Reb Shimon's determination and dedication had paid off. He had earned enough to make Shabbos!

That Friday night, Reb Shimon felt like a king as he sat in his chair at the head of the table, presiding over a modest Shabbos feast in the comfort of his own home. There wasn't much; Gittel had managed to procure a little flour, some potatoes, and a few eggs. She's managed to purchase and *kasher* an extremely scrawny chicken as well. Still, it was enough. The portions may have been meager, but the feeling of independence gave the food an incredible flavoring of richness and satisfaction.

One month passed, then another. Reb Shimon lived for Shabbos. His days were filled with backbreaking drudgery, but he constantly reminded himself that the few extra pennies he earned would enable Gittel to purchase enough staples for their Shabbos meals. His health was beginning to leave him, but he refused to slow down. Now that he had tasted the joy of self-sufficiency, he did not want to find himself forced to rely on the generosity of others ever again.

One day, the village buzzed with excitement. Reb Yidel Schwartz, a wealthy businessman from a nearby town, had come into the village *shul* for *Minchah*. What was he doing here? Could it have anything to do with the rumors of a new business that was going up just outside the village? The men eagerly traded theories, but Reb Shimon did not stop to listen. He was eager to rush back to work, hoping to earn a lit-

tle bit more before he returned home for the night. As Reb Shimon
stepped out of the *shul*, he heard someone call his name. Turning, he
was surprised to see Reb Yidel himself approaching. "*Shalom Ale-
ichem*, Reb Shimon," Reb Yidel said genially. "Could you spare a moment of your time for me?"

"Of course," Reb Shimon said. "What can I do for you?"

"I have heard many good things about you, " Reb Yidel began. "I
made many inquiries before I came here to the village, and everyone
agrees that Reb Shimon Kaplan is an honest, responsible, conscien-
tious worker. I have been looking for someone like you for a long
time, Reb Shimon. I would like to make you an offer."

Reb Shimon was rather taken aback by this. He slaved from dawn
to dark to earn enough money to put food on the table, and a rich man
like Reb Yidel Schwartz wanted to do business with him? "I think
you're making a mistake," he said hesitantly. "I appreciate your compliments, but if you have indeed heard about me, then you surely
must know that I am a very poor man. I couldn't possibly share in an
investment of —"

"No, no, Reb Shimon," Reb Yidel interrupted him with a smile. "You
don't understand. I'm not interested in that. I want to offer you a job!"

"A job?" Reb Shimon repeated.

"Perhaps you've heard of the new project going up just outside the
village?"

Reb Shimon nodded. Everyone had heard of it.

"I purchased the business a few months ago. I'm now in the middle
of construction. As I don't live here in the village, I've been looking for
someone trustworthy who can manage the place for me. I think you're
the man I'm looking for, Reb Shimon. Will you take the job?"

Reb Shimon was speechless. He felt as if the entire world had suddenly been thrust into his hands. The chance for a real, well paying
job seemed too good to be true.

"You understand, it'll take a bit longer before the business is up
and running," Reb Yidel added apologetically. "It will probably be
close to another year before you will be able to begin. but I can promise you a good salary. So, nu, Reb Shimon? What do you say?"

Reb Shimon laughed aloud. "Of course I'll take the job! Thank you, Reb Yidel. I appreciate this, more than I can say."

Reb Yidel smiled and shook hands with Reb Shimon. "We'll be in touch, then. I look forward to working with you."

Reb Shimon practically ran home, bursting to tell Gittel the good news. He had a job! A salaried position, working for a decent, wealthy businessman. How he thanked Hashém for offering him this marvelous change in *mazel*!

For the next several days, Reb Shimon awakened each morning with a smile on his lips. Who cared if they still suffered from the grinding poverty that had characterized their entire life? With Hashem's help, next year, everything would change.

On Thursday, Reb Shimon met Reb Mechel Grossman on the street. "Reb Shimon, congratulations!" Reb Mechel greeted him. "We heard the good news. I'm sure you must be looking forward to starting your new job."

"*Baruch Hashem*," Reb Shimon answered happily. "Reb Yidel tells me that it will still take quite some time before the business is ready to open, but I'm sure that the time will pass quickly."

"Well, in the meantime, would you honor my family by joining us for the Shabbos *seudos* this week?"

Reb Shimon coughed uncomfortably. "Reb Mechel, that is a very kind offer. But you see..."

"Yes?" Reb Mechel looked at him inquiringly.

Reb Shimon flushed, embarrassed. "We really don't eat by other people's homes anymore, "he explained stiffly. "We prefer to eat at home."

"Come, Reb Shimon," Reb Mechel urged. "You can join us. I understand that you sometimes might feel uncomfortable to eat by others, but I assure you that you will feel right at home by us. You know me, Reb Shimon. My wife and I are simple people. We won't try to impress you with fancy fare. Please come. You won't feel out of place."

Reb Shimon mulled this over. It was true that Reb Mechel lived a life as simple as his own. Perhaps he wouldn't feel too uncomfortable after all. "All right," he said at last. "We will come. Thank you very much for your invitation."

Gittel was quite surprised when Reb Shimon told her that he had accepted an invitation to eat their Shabbos meals by Reb Mechel's home. She was secretly relieved. That week had been more difficult than most; it would have been almost impossible to purchase enough for the Shabbos meals. She was glad that her husband had not let his pride get the better of him.

That Shabbos night, Reb Shimon and his family arrived at Reb Mechel's house for the *seudah*. Just as Reb Mechel had promised, the food was plentiful, but simple. Gittel and the children were soon relaxed and comfortable, but Reb Shimon seemed somewhat pensive.

At one point, Reb Mechel leaned over to whisper in his guest's ear. "What is troubling you, Reb Shimon?" he asked quietly. "Have I not kept my word and given you only simple fare?"

"Yes, my friend," Reb Shimon replied. "It is not your fault. I am being ungrateful, I know. Its just that —" He signed. "It is my pride, I suppose. It hurts me to accept an invitation like this, knowing that I cannot provide for my own family. It makes me feel poor."

"Don't feel that way, Reb Shimon," Reb Mechel consoled him. "Don't forget, this won't last long. After all, you are assured of an excellent job that will begin in just a few months. Soon you will be able to provide your family with everything you need. Can't you look at this as something only temporary?"

Reb Shimon smiled and nodded his head. "You are right," he said gratefully. "With Hashem's help, these hardships will soon pass."

Reb Shimon finally relaxed. Reb Mechel was right. His current situation would soon be over. It was only a passing stage. Soon enough, he would be able to support his family in the way they truly deserved.

❖ ❖ ❖

The *Haggadah* begins: " *This is the bread of affliction, which our ancestors ate in the land of Egypt.*" Why do we offer such an ungracious invitation?

These words are directed towards the needy, so that they can come and enjoy the *seder* without feeling any discomfort. The food that is being offered is simple; this is the same *matzah* that we ate in Egypt as slaves, when we all lived in poverty and no one fared better than the next. There is no need to feel awkward at being invited to a meal with such simple food.

מסלקים הקערה עם המצות ומוזגים כוס שני.

מַה נִּשְׁתַּנָּה הַלַּיְלָה הַזֶּה מִכָּל הַלֵּילוֹת.

שֶׁבְּכָל הַלֵּילוֹת אָנוּ אוֹכְלִין חָמֵץ וּמַצָּה. הַלַּיְלָה הַזֶּה כֻּלּוֹ מַצָּה:

שֶׁבְּכָל הַלֵּילוֹת אָנוּ אוֹכְלִין שְׁאָר יְרָקוֹת. הַלַּיְלָה הַזֶּה (כֻּלּוֹ) מָרוֹר:

שֶׁבְּכָל הַלֵּילוֹת אֵין אָנוּ מַטְבִּילִין אֲפִילוּ פַּעַם אֶחָת. הַלַּיְלָה הַזֶּה שְׁתֵּי פְעָמִים:

שֶׁבְּכָל הַלֵּילוֹת אָנוּ אוֹכְלִין בֵּין יוֹשְׁבִין וּבֵין מְסֻבִּין. הַלַּיְלָה הַזֶּה כֻּלָּנוּ מְסֻבִּין:

יחזיר הקערה לפניו עם המצות ויקרא כל ההגדה

עֲבָדִים הָיִינוּ לְפַרְעֹה בְּמִצְרַיִם. וַיּוֹצִיאֵנוּ יְיָ אֱלֹהֵינוּ מִשָּׁם בְּיָד חֲזָקָה וּבִזְרֹעַ נְטוּיָה. וְאִלּוּ לֹא הוֹצִיא הַקָּדוֹשׁ בָּרוּךְ הוּא אֶת אֲבוֹתֵינוּ מִמִּצְרַיִם. הֲרֵי אָנוּ וּבָנֵינוּ וּבְנֵי בָנֵינוּ מְשֻׁעְבָּדִים הָיִינוּ לְפַרְעֹה בְּמִצְרָיִם. וַאֲפִילוּ כֻּלָּנוּ חֲכָמִים. כֻּלָּנוּ נְבוֹנִים. כֻּלָּנוּ זְקֵנִים. כֻּלָּנוּ יוֹדְעִים אֶת הַתּוֹרָה. מִצְוָה עָלֵינוּ לְסַפֵּר בִּיצִיאַת מִצְרָיִם. וְכָל הַמַּרְבֶּה לְסַפֵּר בִּיצִיאַת מִצְרַיִם הֲרֵי זֶה מְשֻׁבָּח.

However, if the guests still feel uneasy at eating at other people's homes, the *Haggadah* offers further words of comfort: the present situation is only temporary. *"This year we are here; next year, may we be in Eretz Yisrael,"* where all Jews will be wealthy under the sheltering wings of Hashem and serve him equally.

Why is this night different from all other nights? ...

The *Baal Haggadah* begins the reply to these four questions with *Avodim Hayinu:*

"We were slaves ... had the Holy Blessed One not taken our ancestors out ... we would still be enslaved to Pharaoh in Egypt..."

Remove the seder plate and pour the second cup.

hy is this night different from all other nights? On all other nights, we eat chametz (leaven) or matzah. On this night, only matzah.

On all other nights, we eat any type of vegetables. On this night, we eat maror (bitter herbs).

On all other nights, we are not required to dip even once. On this night, we dip twice.

On all other nights, we eat either sitting upright or re-clining. On this night, we all recline.

Replace the Ke'arah and say the rest of the Haggadah.

e were slaves to Pharaoh in Egypt, but Hashem our G-d, brought us out from there with a strong hand and an outstretched arm. Had the Holy Blessed One not taken our ancestors out of Egypt, then we, our children and our grandchildren would still be en-slaved to Pharaoh in Egypt. Therefore even if we were all wise, all men of understanding, all elders, all knowledge-able in Torah, we would still be commanded to tell about the Exodus from Egypt. And whoever tells about it at length deserves to be praised.

Why must the answer to these questions add that if Hashem had not taken us out of Egypt, we and our descendants would still be en-slaved? How does this observation explain why this night of Pesach is different from all other nights of the year?

❉ ❉ ❉

Velvel had made up his mind. The journey might be perilous and uncertain, but living in their hometown was no longer a possibility. One way or another, Velvel was determined to take his wife and children and begin life anew across the sea.

His loyal wife packed their meager belongings as they prepared for the long trip. The children were excited at the prospect of a long journey by boat, sailing across the vast ocean to see foreign shores. They had no concept of the many dangers that might await them.

Many of Velvel's neighbors and friends tried to dissuade him from such a perilous venture, arguing that the risks were not worth the possible benefits.

"Don't be a fool, Velvel," they warned him. "Life may be difficult for the Jews here, but who is to say that it will be any better where you are going? And how can you be certain that you'll get there at all? If your ship's captain is unscrupulous, he may demand additional bribes to set you down where you want to go; you can run into stormy weather, or even pirates! Stay where it's safe, Velvel! Better an uneasy life than no life at all!"

Velvel refused to listen to these dire warnings. "It is time for us to move on," he asserted quietly. "Hashem will guide our lives across the ocean, just as He does here."

The day of their scheduled departure arrived. Many of their friends and relatives accompanied Velvel's family to the shore. The children lined up along the rail of the sturdy ship, waving excitedly at their friends and cousins standing on the dock.

"Good-bye, good-bye!" the children cried. "Remember us!"

"*Tzeischem l'shalom!*" their family and neighbors called back. "Travel in health and safety!"

With the creaking of hawsers and the booming of sails, the ship turned into the wind and moved steadily away from the shore. Velvel and his family were on their way.

At first, the children found the trip exciting. They spent hours and hours on deck, watching the long swells of water as the ship plowed steadily through the waves. The bracing air and fresh breeze were exhilarating, and they could barely be coaxed into the family's cabin for meals.

As the days passed, however, the long journey became more and more monotonous. The children began to mope, spending more and more time below deck with their parents. What had once seemed fresh and exciting had become dull and boring.

They had been sailing for sixteen days when the boring journey suddenly became all too exciting. Only one of Velvel's children was above deck when the ship's crew spotted the black sails of five ships, still some distance away. Quickly, the sailors sent all the passengers down below, refusing to answer any questions.

"What's happening?" Velvel's wife asked with anxiety.

"Yankel saw ships approaching," Velvel said quietly. "Let us pray to Hashem that their intentions are peaceful..."

Such hopes were soon crushed. The passengers huddled in their cabins for hours, quaking with terror at the sounds of shouting and fighting from above. The sudden silence that fell upon the ship only made things worse.

Then the door of their cabin was flung open. A uniformed soldier stood framed in the doorway.

"Out!" the soldier barked in a guttural accent. "On to the deck!"

Velvel kept a reassuring hand on his youngest son's shoulder as he quietly followed the soldier up to the main deck. There, they saw the other passengers gathered together at the stern, their hands tied together. The last shreds of hope vanished as Velvel realized that he and his family were now prisoners.

"We're telling you this only once," the enemy captain shouted as a soldier tied Velvel's hands together with a bit of rope. "Anyone who misbehaves will be shot instantly. We won't waste food and water on rebellious prisoners. You're our slaves now, and if you want to live, you'll do as you're told!"

"Do as he says," Velvel whispered to his wife and children. "For now, we must do our best to survive. We must trust in Hashem that we will remain unharmed."

"Now, we are sending you all back to your cabins," their captor continued. "You may not leave the cabins for any reason without permission. Remember, we will shoot you at once if you disobey!"

The long, harrowing nightmare began. Velvel and his family spent long, dreary days in their cramped cabin, aching for a breath of fresh air or a bite of something more than old, stale bread. They did not dare to even open their cabin door, feeling too frightened of their captors to risk their anger. Only the solace of the Torah they could review and the Tehillim they could recite prevented them from going insane.

At last, they were ordered on deck and led to the gangway. Pale, dirty, and gaunt from lack of food, the prisoners stumbled as they hurried to keep up with the soldiers. Velvel looked bleakly at the sight before him: a small string of islands in the middle of nowhere. This was their new "home."

The captain, looking well fed and arrayed in a fresh-pressed uniform, awaited them on shore.

"You are all slaves now," he began without preamble. "Accept your fates, for this is your home for eternity. However, if you work loyally and earnestly, you will find that you are treated well. Families will be allowed to stay together; you will be granted sufficient food and drink."

The captain continued, but Velvel no longer listened. He exchanged glances with his wife, then looked at his children. He could not protect them from slavery, but he would do everything in his power to make sure that he and his family remained loyal Torah Jews.

The years passed slowly. Velvel's family had grown used to their new routine: a long day's labor in the fields, then the blessed peace of evenings at home together. Their children grew older; new children were born. Velvel continued to encourage his family to keep whatever *mitzvos* they could. This constant reminder of their status as Jews also helped them recall the happy days before they'd become slaves. At times, those memories of freedom seemed little more than a dream, but they never stopped praying to Hashem for redemption.

One evening, as Velvel's family trudged through the fields, they heard a sudden tumult of shouting and fighting. Frightened, Velvel snatched up their youngest child and led the way as he ran towards the sanctuary of their little house. For long hours, they remained huddled together, listening to the sounds of fighting in the distance. Velvel could not help remembering how similar the noises had been on that fateful day, so many years ago, when they had been captured at sea.

At last, the sounds of fighting died away. For several minutes, no matter how hard they concentrated, they could hear nothing. Then a new noise started: cheering and laughter! Velvel crept out of the room and peeked cautiously around the door frame. There, a short distance away, several slaves were laughing and dancing together. Velvel froze at the sight. If their masters caught them, they would surely be killed!

One of the men caught sight of Velvel. "Join us!" he shouted exuberantly. "We are free! We have been liberated!"

Velvel hesitated. Could it really be true?

"We are free!" the man shouted again, grinning from ear to ear. "Our masters have been defeated, and their conquerors have said that we are all free to go!"

Velvel waited no longer. Shouting the joyous news to his wife, he raced to join the whirling circle of men celebrating their newfound freedom.

Events moved quickly after that. Within a few months, Velvel and his family found themselves newly settled in the country that had been their original destination, so many years before. With a good-paying job and a nice home, Velvel's family was finally at peace.

Velvel never forgot the miracle of his redemption from slavery. Every year, on the anniversary of his release, he and his entire family gathered together. With praises to Hashem on their lips, they partook in a joyous meal to commemorate their personal miracle.

Years turned into decades. Velvel merited to see most of his grandchildren marry before he died peacefully in his sleep in his mid-eighties. His loyal wife survived him by only a few weeks. With their passing, the family grew less close-knit, but all of their descendants remained faithful to the Torah and the lessons that Velvel had taught them. Only one thing had fallen by the wayside: the *seudas hoda'ah,* the special festive meal with which Velvel had celebrated the day they had been released from slavery.

One day, a grandchild met Berel, an elderly gentleman who had been a close friend of Velvel for many years.

"Reb Berel!" the young man greeted his grandfather's friend. "How nice to see you!"

"How is little Velvel?" Berel smiled. "How wonderful to have a child named after your honored grandfather!"

מַעֲשֶׂה בְּרַבִּי אֱלִיעֶזֶר וְרַבִּי יְהוֹשֻׁעַ וְרַבִּי אֶלְעָזָר בֶּן עֲזַרְיָה וְרַבִּי
עֲקִיבָא וְרַבִּי טַרְפוֹן שֶׁהָיוּ מְסֻבִּין בִּבְנֵי בְרַק וְהָיוּ
מְסַפְּרִים בִּיצִיאַת מִצְרַיִם כָּל אוֹתוֹ הַלַּיְלָה עַד שֶׁבָּאוּ תַלְמִידֵיהֶם
וְאָמְרוּ לָהֶם. רַבּוֹתֵינוּ הִגִּיעַ זְמַן קְרִיאַת שְׁמַע שֶׁל שַׁחֲרִית.

After a few minutes of conversation, Berel peered at the younger man and said, "You know, I am somewhat surprised at your family. I was rather disappointed to see that you have failed to keep your grandfather's custom of commemorating your family's redemption from slavery. It meant so much to Velvel. Why did you stop?"

The grandson, taken aback, merely shrugged. "I know Grandfather took it seriously, but really, Reb Berel, what does it have to do with me? My father was only five years old when the family was freed. It was long before I was born. Why should I celebrate something that has nothing to do with me?"

"You are wrong," Berel corrected gently. "Don't you realize that when your grandfather and his family were taken as prisoners, they were told that they would be slaves for eternity? Your father was born there, you know. If he and your grandparents had not been rescued from slavery, you would have been born there as well. In fact, you would still be there, now, working in the fields. Don't you see? It was not only your father and grandfather that were redeemed, but you, your children, and all of your future generations! Your little Velvel, your pride and joy — he, too, would be a slave if your family had not been redeemed! So you see, my friend, you really still must make that *seudas hoda'ah* and thank Hashem for freeing you from slavery."

❊ ❊ ❊

The crucial word of the four questions is "we." Why must we eat *matzah, maror* and dip twice? Why must we recline? We were not slaves in Egypt!

The *Baal Haggadah* explains this by answering, "Had the Holy One, Blessed Be He, not taken our ancestors out of Egypt, then we, our children and our children's children would still

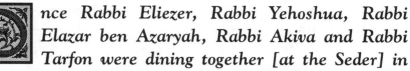

nce Rabbi Eliezer, Rabbi Yehoshua, Rabbi Elazar ben Azaryah, Rabbi Akiva and Rabbi Tarfon were dining together [at the Seder] in Bnei Brak. They discussed the Exodus from Egypt throughout the entire night until their students came and told them: "Teachers, it is time to recite the morning Shema."

be enslaved to Pharaoh in Egypt..." We commemorate this night because we do, indeed, have something to celebrate.

Once Rabbi Eliezer ... were dining together [at the Seder] in Bnei Brak ..."

The recounting of this episode adds weight to the previous statement that, "Even if we are all wise, all men of understanding, all elders, all knowledgeable in Torah, we are still commanded to relate the Exodus from Egypt..."

Why is it so important to stress that even the sages fulfilled this particular *mitzvah*? Aren't all the commandments of the Torah incumbent on every single individual?

Reb Hirsch looked up as his servant appeared in the doorway of his study. "Excuse me, sir," the man said deferentially, "there is a Mr. Berg here to see you. He says that he is in need of your assistance."

"But of course," Reb Hirsch replied, laying his business papers aside. "Please, send him in immediately."

Reb Hirsch was used to such visits. With his vast wealth and personal friendship with the king, he was in an excellent position to intercede for his fellow Jews. Unlike many other rich men, who often ignored others and concentrated solely on their own whims, Reb Hirsch devoted a great deal of time and effort towards helping those in need.

Mr. Berg entered the study. His suit was clearly worn, but he was neat and presentable. Only his eyes betrayed his desperation.

"Reb Hirsch," he said, his voice barely above a whisper. "I need your help. My entire family is at risk."

"Tell me how I can help you," Reb Hirsch soothed him. "Please, sit down, and I will do everything I can to be of assistance."

"It's the tax collectors," Mr. Berg sighed, sinking into a chair. "What can I tell you, Reb Hirsch? Hashem has not seen fit to bless me with money or business acumen. I earn enough to keep my wife and children warm and fed, but I have no savings. If my expenses suddenly go up, there is no way I can manage."

"I don't understand," Reb Hirsch frowned. "What does this have to do with the tax collectors?"

Mr. Berg gave a bitter laugh. "Well, they wouldn't have tried it with you, I suppose. You are too powerful, too close to the king. But I know it's happened to many others. And now they threaten to take the roof from over my children's heads!"

"Mr. Berg," Reb Hirsch said patiently, "you still haven't told me what the problem is. Perhaps you could speak more clearly?"

Mr. Berg flushed. "I'm sorry, Reb Hirsch. I'll try to be more specific." He paused for a moment, arranging his thoughts. "As you know, the king appoints certain men to collect the taxes. The same people are responsible year after year, and it looks like the power of the position has gone to their heads. When they came to collect the king's due, they were not satisfied with the usual amount."

"What do you mean?" Reb Hirsch leaned forward.

"I mean, Reb Hirsch, that the officials have been raising the tax amounts by themselves! They are putting that extra money in their own pockets. And if I don't pay them by tomorrow, they've threatened to take my home and livelihood as payment instead!" Mr. Berg wrung his hands. "Reb Hirsch, what should I do? If they take my store and my house away, how will my family and I survive?"

Reb Hirsch sat back in his leather chair, lost in thought. This revelation of corruption in the government ranks was a shocking one. He knew the king to be a man who genuinely cared for his subjects and administered strict justice. Could it be that the king was simply unaware of what his officials were doing?

"The tax officials don't pay the tax themselves, either," Mr. Berg added moodily. "They pay nothing for themselves, and expect to get more money out of me!" He flushed again. "I suppose I have to admit, Reb Hirsch, that I've been a little lax myself in that respect. I could have paid off the tax over the past year, a little bit at a time; but when I saw the attitude of the tax collectors, I guess I didn't take the tax seriously myself. Now I have to suffer the consequences." He put his head in his hands. "Not only must I pay a year's tax at once, but the collectors are demanding even more money. There's no way I can pay it! I'm going to lose everything I have!"

"Please, Mr. Berg, let me think for a moment." Reb Hirsch sat in silence, stroking his beard thoughtfully. "I'll tell you what," he said at last. "I believe I have an idea, but I must plan for all contingencies. Could you come back in a few hours?" He looked carefully at the man's threadbare suit. "If you could arrive at one o'clock, perhaps you could join us for dinner," he added casually.

Mr. Berg rose from his chair, shaking Reb Hirsch's hand gratefully. "Thank you, Reb Hirsch. I will return at one o'clock."

After Mr. Berg left, Reb Hirsch took several sheets of paper and began to scribble down his thoughts. For over an hour he sat there, thinking hard, crossing out notes and writing new ones. At last, he was satisfied that his plan would work — if the king was willing to listen.

When Mr. Berg returned, Reb Hirsch refused to reveal any details of his plan. "You have nothing to worry about, Mr. Berg," he assured him. "All you need to do is tell the collectors to come to me."

"I don't understand."

"When the officials come to your business tomorrow, tell them to come to me," Reb Hirsch repeated. "Tell them that I will handle your obligations. I will take care of the payment."

"But — but –" Mr. Berg tried to protest. "I can't let you –"

"Just leave it to me, Mr. Berg." Reb Hirsch smiled at the anxious man." I'll take care of the rest."

Mr. Berg went home and spent the rest of the day — and the entire night — worrying.

The following morning, the dreaded knocking on the door began. "Open up, in the name of the king!" a voice called.

Trembling, Mr. Berg opened the door. Four men, dressed in imposing uniforms, stood on his doorstep. "Reuvein Berg," one man said sternly, "we have come to collect the taxes that you, as a loyal citizen, owe your king. Do you have it ready?"

"I — I cannot pay you," Mr. Berg quavered.

The official's eyes narrowed. He stepped forward menacingly. "In that case..."

"Wait!" Mr. Berg said desperately. "Sir Hirsch! Sir Hirsch told me to tell you that he will pay my taxes for me!"

The four men exchanged glances. "These Jews are more foolish than I thought," one said at last. "Very well, Jew. We will go see Sir Hirsch. I hope for your sake that you are telling the truth!"

Moments later, the tax collectors were knocking on the door of Reb Hirsch's imposing home. "Inform Sir Hirsch that the king's tax officials are here," they barked.

As soon as they entered Reb Hirsch's elegant study, however, the officials changed their tune. They knew Reb Hirsch was a personal friend of the king, and his wealth was evident from his home. This was no poor Jew they could bully, but a man who deserved their respect.

"Excuse us, sir," the head official said politely. "We have been told that you are willing to pay Reuvein Berg's taxes. Is this true?"

"It was," Reb Hirsch said carelessly.

"Excuse me?"

"I was going to pay his taxes," Reb Hirsch explained, "but I won't. I won't pay my taxes, either. Not this year. Not ever."

"B-but, sir!" the man spluttered. "You can't do that?"

"Why not?" Reb Hirsch retorted. "You and the rest of the tax officials don't pay taxes, do you?"

"Of course not!" the official said proudly. "We have been appointed by the king himself! We are some of the most high-ranking officers in the kingdom. Why should we have to pay?"

"Then I won't pay, either," Reb Hirsch said with finality. He picked up a silver bell from his desk and shook it. In moments, his servant appeared in the doorway.

"Escort these gentlemen out of the house," he instructed. "They are not to come back."

The bewildered tax officials found themselves standing outside Reb Hirsch's home, confused by the sudden turn of events. After a few minutes, however, they began to become angry.

"No one can get away with this kind of behavior!" one of them exclaimed. "Come! We must report this to the king."

The king listened to the officials' report in silence. "You must imprison him, Your Majesty!" the head collector declared. "This is an affront to your throne!"

The king, however, was a little wiser than his officials might have thought. "I will see him myself," he declared. "Summon him to the palace immediately."

When Reb Hirsch arrived, he bowed deeply and respectfully to his ruler. "How may I serve His Majesty?" he asked softly.

"You may explain what happened this morning," the king replied dryly. "Why did you tell my officials that you will no longer pay my taxes?"

"Your Majesty, there is no other subject in your kingdom who honors and respects your rule as I do," Reb Hirsch began. "I assure you, I have every intention of meeting my obligations to the throne. Unfortunately, I have discovered a lack of loyalty among your own officers."

"What do you mean?" the king demanded.

Reb Hirsch recounted the tale of the tax collectors and Mr. Berg. "They have begun to raise the taxes Your Majesty; not for the benefit of the crown, but for themselves."

The king absorbed this shocking news. "I will not tolerate this," he said grimly. "They must be imprisoned for their betrayal of my trust!"

"If I may make a suggestion, Your Majesty?" Reb Hirsch said deferentially.

The king looked at the Jew with some amusement. Reb Hirsch had often proved his cleverness in the past. "Go ahead," he replied.

"Your Majesty," Reb Hirsch said in a tone of great earnestness, "it seems to me that this laxity is due to the officials' own exemption

אָמַר רַבִּי אֶלְעָזָר בֶּן עֲזַרְיָה. הֲרֵי אֲנִי כְּבֶן שִׁבְעִים שָׁנָה. וְלֹא זָכִיתִי שֶׁתֵּאָמֵר יְצִיאַת מִצְרַיִם בַּלֵּילוֹת. עַד שֶׁדְּרָשָׁהּ בֶּן זוֹמָא שֶׁנֶּאֱמַר לְמַעַן תִּזְכֹּר אֶת יוֹם צֵאתְךָ מֵאֶרֶץ מִצְרַיִם כָּל יְמֵי חַיֶּיךָ. יְמֵי חַיֶּיךָ הַיָּמִים. כֹּל יְמֵי חַיֶּיךָ הַלֵּילוֹת. וַחֲכָמִים אוֹמְרִים. יְמֵי חַיֶּיךָ הָעוֹלָם הַזֶּה. כֹּל יְמֵי חַיֶּיךָ לְהָבִיא לִימוֹת הַמָּשִׁיחַ.

from taxes. I know that the original reasoning was that those who worked in the government need not pay taxes, since they spent all their time working for the throne; but I am afraid this only leads to corruption. If they themselves do not pay taxes, it is easy for them to treat those same taxes without respect. I believe, Your Majesty, that if your officials were required to pay taxes, they would treat their responsibilities with the same respect as do your other subjects."

"I see…"

"There is more, Your Majesty," Reb Hirsch added. "If regular citizens see that the government officials are paying their taxes, they will realize its importance. I am sure that you would see an improvement in attitude throughout the kingdom."

The king smiled. "You have made your point. I agree with you. From now on, everyone will be required to pay taxes, no matter what responsibilities they hold. If the officials also pay taxes, it will be an example for all."

❈ ❈ ❈

The *Baal Haggadah* emphasizes that everyone is required to relate the story of the Exodus from Egypt, even the sages. No matter how high one's level of faith and piety might be, every single Jew is still obligated to keep all the commandments of the Torah. Although Rabbi Eliezer, Rabbi Yehoshua, Rabbi Elazar ben Azaryah, Rabbi Akiva, and Rabbi Tarfon were towering Torah sages, they not only fulfilled their obligation, but they even stayed up the entire night in performance of this *mitzvah*!

abbi Elazar ben Azaryah said: Behold, I am like a seventy-year-old man, and I was not fortunate enough to show that the Exodus must be recited at night until ben Zoma interpreted the verse: "In order that you remember the day you left Egypt all the days of your life," the days; [adding the word] "all" includes the nights. The Sages interpreted [the verse] "the days of your life" refers to the present world; "all the days of your life" indicates the Messianic era.

Rabbi Elazar ben Azaryah said: Behold I am like a seventy-year-old man ...

The *gemara* in *Berachos* relates that Rabbi Elazar ben Azaryah was actually only eighteen years of age when he was appointed as *Nasi*, but he was accorded the same respect as a seventy-year-old man. Why, then, could he not prove his teaching that the Exodus must be recited at night until Ben Zoma interpreted the verse of the Torah?

Yitzchak paced up and down the gleaming marble hallway, fighting down panic. Why, oh, why had he spoken so brashly? The people he most wanted to impress would arrive in less than an hour, and he had nothing to tell them!

He thought back to that heady moment a few days ago, when the directors of Klein's Industrial Diamonds had informed him that they were ready to hire him.

"Your credentials are impeccable, young man," the senior director told him. "You have the knowledge, the insight, and the experience that we're looking for. You realize, of course, that it's a big job; we can't just have you start managing our main production plant without a trial run first. Let's give it two weeks, Yitzchak. If you work out well, then the job is yours."

Yitzchak shook hands with the man, feeling dazed. Could it possibly be true? Was he really about to begin the job of his dreams? "I won't disappoint you, Mr. Klein," he managed to say. "You'll see!"

He walked out of the directors' boardroom, almost giddy with excitement. At last! The chance to prove himself had finally arrived!

He'd worked so hard to reach this point, but he'd been fighting one major drawback for several years now: he was too young. No one wanted to trust a man in his mid-twenties with major responsibilities, no matter how bright and industrious he might be. Time and time again, he'd lost the opportunity for promotion simply because of his age. Now, at last, he had the chance to prove, once and for all, that he was truly capable!

Yitzchak got right to work. He prowled through the halls of the vast plant, exploring and examining things up close. He was already familiar with the process; he'd done his homework before he applied for the job. But the chance to see things up close excited him. He already had several ideas; ideas that would make the directors sit up and take notice.

He presented his idea to his superiors on the following day. "As you know, Klein's Industrial Diamonds specializes in practical applications for diamonds in industrial use," he began. "Of course, the final products use diamonds in such small amounts that their intrinsic value is useless; it's the application that makes our products worthwhile. However, we do need diamonds in large amounts to begin production, and that's where we have a major roadblock in our budget."

"What do you mean?" one of the directors asked.

"The diamonds are sent to us by courier," Yitzchak reminded him, "a courier who is accompanied by at least two bodyguards. The diamonds in transit are also heavily insured. Transporting the diamonds is expensive — needlessly so."

"But how can we arrange for the diamonds to be brought to us in a cheaper manner?" another man protested. "If we don't have adequate security, the diamonds might not arrive here at all!"

"If the diamonds are shipped in a more discreet fashion, there would be no need for bodyguards. We might not even have to pay those outrageous insurance charges. Over the course of the year, this would save the company tens of thousands of dollars."

There was a moment of silence as the directors considered Yitzchak's words. "It seems like a sound idea, Yitzchak," Mr. Klein finally said. "But how do you plan on shipping the diamonds 'discreetly'? How can you be sure that the shipment won't be at risk?"

Yitzchak, eager to win Mr. Klein's approval, quickly replied, "That's not a problem, sir. It would be quite simple. It just takes a little imagination to come up with a solid plan. I'll present you with a full outline by tomorrow morning."

"Excellent," Mr. Klein smiled. "I look forward to hearing your proposal."

Yitzchak walked out of the room with a jaunty stride, fighting to keep the grin off his face. He'd impressed his employers! Now he just had to keep it up and —

Suddenly, it all came crashing down on him. What had he done? He'd just promised Mr. Klein a full-fledged plan for safe, cheap transport of the diamonds by tomorrow morning. But how? No matter how airily he'd spoken of the need for just a "little imagination," he didn't dare present the directors with anything less than a sensible, workable proposal. What was he going to do now?

Yitzchak did not sleep that night. He dreamed up ideas, thought them brilliant for several moments, and then, in despair, discarded them as useless. Hide the diamonds in false-bottomed crates — and be arrested for smuggling? Ridiculous! Skip the insurance? That would mean short-term savings, but one slip-up would cost the company thousands of dollars — and probably his job as well! What in the world would he tell Mr. Klein in the morning?

"And here I am," Yitzchak said aloud in despair. He had one short hour before his daily meeting with the directors, sixty minutes before he was supposed to meet his employers and present them with a "simple" plan to save the company thousands of dollars every year. And he had no idea what he was going to say to them!"

"I can't believe I was such a fool," he whispered to himself. With a few rash words, Yitzchak had thrown away everything he'd accomplished over the past few years. There was no way in the world that the directors would extend his contract beyond the two-week trial period. How could they trust him, when he made grand statements and then failed to give his theories any backing?

Moodily, Yitzchak left the gracefully appointed office and made his way towards the more austere buildings where the real work was accomplished. He walked up and down the aisles, observing the workers and encouraging their efforts. Despite his feelings of gloom, he forced himself to smile pleasantly and hide his despair.

He must not have been doing a very good job, because one young boy who worked in the packaging department looked at him rather strangely. "Is everything all right, sir?" the boy asked hesitantly.

"Yes, yes, of course," Yitzchak said quickly. "Carry on."

He made his rounds through the rest of the packaging department, then prepared to leave. He was surprised to see the same boy waiting for him by the door.

"Can I help you…" With an effort, Yitzchak remembered the boy's name. "…Ephraim?"

"Uh, actually, sir," the boy stammered, "I was hoping I could help *you.*"

"What do you mean?"

Ephraim took a deep breath. "Sir, you've come to visit the department many times in the last few days, and I know that something's troubling you. I just wanted to know if I could help out, that's all."

Yitzchak summoned up a smile. "That's very kind of you, Ephraim, but I don't think you would be able to help me."

"Sir, don't look down on me because I'm young," Ephraim stated quietly. "Why don't you try asking me? Perhaps I can help, after all."

Yitzchak was taken aback. Was he treating Ephraim the same way he'd been treated himself — ignored because of his young age? "It's kind of you," Yitzchak said slowly, "but I really don't think you can help. You see, I'm trying to come up with a way to allow the company to transport the diamonds we need without the necessity of armed guards and expensive insurance."

Ephraim brightened. "Oh, that's easy!"

Yitzchak stared at him. "Excuse me? Did you say easy?"

"Oh, sure!" Ephraim said. "I read a story about something like that a couple of months ago. A merchant had to carry a packet of jewels from one country to another without any guards. He was afraid of thieves, so he dressed himself in rags and made sure that he smelled disgusting. Everybody thought he was a beggar without two coins to rub together, so robbers left him alone. Maybe you could do something like that, too!"

Yitzchak was thunderstruck. The idea was so simple — and that was the beauty of it! A courier, dressed in an expensive suit, was an obvious target that needed bodyguards; but a drunken beggar? He could carry the priceless diamonds in a filthy, old bag, and no one would be the wiser! If he could find a trustworthy messenger with a flair for acting, perhaps the idea would really work!

"Ephraim," he finally managed to say, "thank you. Thank you very much. I'm going to see what the directors think of your idea." Turning, he half-ran out the door and hurried back to the office building. The directors would be waiting for him, and at last he had something to tell them!

Mr. Klein, seated at the head of the mahogany table in the boardroom, looked up as Yitzchak entered. "Good morning, Yitzchak," he said. "What do you have to report today?"

Yitzchak stood straight. "Gentlemen, yesterday I suggested that we might find a way for the company to transport diamonds in a less expensive fashion. I believe I have a proposal that just might suit us."

"Go on," Mr. Klein urged, looking intrigued.

"The key to my plan is preventing the diamonds from becoming a target in the first place. If we send a messenger by third class instead of first, dressed in worn-out clothing instead of the latest in suits, why would anyone think to rob him? Add a bottle of whiskey to the picture and an offensive odor, and no one would even get close to our messenger — much less find the diamonds he was carrying!"

As Yitzchak spoke, he looked anxiously from one face to another. Each of the directors looked thoughtful and interested. Did they think the idea was worthwhile?

"I like it," one man murmured.

"Seems promising," another director agreed.

בָּרוּךְ הַמָּקוֹם. בָּרוּךְ הוּא. בָּרוּךְ שֶׁנָּתַן תּוֹרָה לְעַמּוֹ יִשְׂרָאֵל.
בָּרוּךְ הוּא. כְּנֶגֶד אַרְבָּעָה בָנִים דִּבְּרָה תוֹרָה. אֶחָד חָכָם.
וְאֶחָד רָשָׁע. וְאֶחָד תָּם. וְאֶחָד שֶׁאֵינוֹ יוֹדֵעַ לִשְׁאוֹל.

"You've really used your imagination, Yitzchak," Mr. Klein added. "Give us a day or two to discuss it, and we'll get back to you." He glanced down at his notebook. "Now, I'd like to ask you about —"

"Just a moment, sir," Yitzchak interrupted. He hadn't wanted to mention it at first, afraid that they would instantly dismiss any suggestion that they knew came from a young boy. "I have to tell you the truth, Mr. Klein. The idea isn't really mine."

"Oh?" Mr. Klein raised his eyebrows.

Yitzchak swallowed. "I was talking to Ephraim Mandelbaum in the packaging department. The idea was his."

The silence lasted much longer this time.

"I see," Mr. Klein said at last. "All right, Yitzchak. We'll talk about it later."

The following morning, Yitzchak was summoned to the office well ahead of time. He entered Mr. Klein's private domain with a sense of apprehension. What was going to happen?

Mr. Klein got straight to the point. "Congratulations, Yitzchak! You're hired on a permanent basis. My secretary has prepared the contract for you. All you have to do is sign on the dotted line."

"But — but —" Yitzchak stammered. He was ready to scream with joy, but he couldn't understand the reason for his sudden good fortune. "What made you...?"

"What made me decide to forgo the rest of the trial period?" Mr. Klein finished for him. "You did, Yitzchak. We wanted to observe you for two weeks to find out whether you're a steady, regular worker, or merely a boy wonder with too much impulsiveness to be trustworthy. Your plan to save us money was a good one, Yitzchak; but that's not what made up my mind. It's the fact that you were honest

lessed be Hashem; blessed be He. Blessed be He who has given His Torah to His nation, Israel; blessed be He. The Torah speaks of four sons: one wise, one wicked, one simple and one who does not know how to ask.

enough to give credit where credit was due. That tells me that you're a man worthy of trust."

Mr. Klein leaned across the desk to shake Yitzchak's hand. "Congratulations, young man. I look forward to working together with you for a long, long time."

Rabbi Elazar ben Azaryah, one of the great sages mentioned in the previous paragraph of the *Haggadah*, was convinced that one is obligated to retell the story of the Exodus at night; but he needed a source as proof. Only a specific verse from the Torah would confirm his teaching. Despite the respect he was accorded, it was only when Ben Zoma found a source in the words, "All the days of your life," that Rabbi Elazar's teaching was accepted. Rabbi Elazar rejoiced in the acceptance of his teaching, and in his humility, he was delighted to grant credit to Ben Zoma for finding the source. It was the concept that mattered, not the credit.

Blessed be Hashem; blessed be He ... one wise, one wicked, one simple and one who does not know how to ask.

What prompted the *Baal Haggadah* to specifically mention Hashem's praise at this point, as well as our good fortune that He gave the "four sons" His Torah?

The king smiled with intense satisfaction as he regarded the device that had demanded such effort and labor for so many months. Unlike other rulers, the King of Marentak truly cared for the welfare of his subjects. He guided his kingdom with a stern hand and the utmost discipline, but he constantly sought ways to better the people's quality of life and increase their education.

Now, in an effort to cultivate scholarship and literacy, the king had invented a device that would provide educational entertainment for his people. Even as they enjoyed themselves, they would find themselves stimulated to increase their thinking and achieve ever-higher levels. The king's eyes sparkled in anticipation of the great benefit his subjects would enjoy from his new invention.

He called in several engineers and explained the device to them, showing them the design and the components required to manufacture the device in quantity. Soon, great numbers of the new invention became widely available, and the people of the capital city rushed to be the first ones to own and use the king's new device.

At first, the King of Marentak was highly pleased with the people's reaction to his device and the increased level of activity. Then he began to receive disturbing information, hints that the invention was not working exactly as he had planned:

"My son can't manage it. It's too complicated for him."

"He tried to use it, but the others only laughed when he couldn't figure it out."

"She can't understand how to play. The level is simply too high for her."

"The other men sit around and discuss it, and my husband is too ashamed to admit that he can't even figure out how to get it started."

The king felt highly disturbed at these reports that filtered into the palace. He hadn't intended for his device to be beyond the capabilities of some of his subjects; and he certainly didn't want those that couldn't handle his invention to be subjected to ridicule and derision by their more intelligent peers! No, something would have to be done to improve his device so that it could be used in the way that he had originally intended.

He took his invention, pulled it apart, and started putting it back together again. This time, however, he added a new feature: several different levels of difficulty, ranging from the most simplistic to the highest ranges of sophistication and subtlety. Then he called back the engineers, instructed them to add the new feature to the device, and sat back to see what would happen.

This time, the king was delighted to see that he had succeeded beyond his wildest dreams! The device could now be used by every single person in the kingdom, no matter how educated or ignorant they might be. The youngest children and the simpler adults could enjoy it on the easiest levels, while the more intelligent and advanced people found themselves constantly challenged to improve. How delighted the king felt when a simple child struggled to overcome his limitations and managed to reach the next level of his invention!

Each person, according to his or her talents, was stimulated and encouraged by the king's invention to think, to produce and to reach ever-higher levels of fulfillment.

Hashem, in His great kindness and love for *Klal Yisrael*, gave every single one of us the priceless gift of His holy Torah. There are no exceptions or exemptions due to intelligence or lack thereof. A person who constantly labors to improve himself, ignoring his limitations, will be treated with great esteem in the eyes of his Creator. In fact, Hashem values such a person more than those that have been blessed with great potential, but are content to rest on the laurels of their own knowledge without ever achieving more.

The *Baal Haggadah* mentions this point to illustrate the preceding paragraph. R' Elazar ben Azaryah, who had been gifted with great brilliance from a young age, still needed the Torah of others to defend and prove his own teachings. R' Elazar's Torah statements were proven as a reward for his great piety; but those other Torah sages, who may have been initially less gifted than he, were the ones who merited to prove those statements as a result of their own labors in Torah.

חָכָם מָה הוּא אוֹמֵר. מָה הָעֵדֹת וְהַחֻקִּים וְהַמִּשְׁפָּטִים אֲשֶׁר צִוָּה
יי אֱלֹהֵינוּ אֶתְכֶם. וְאַף אַתָּה אֱמָר לוֹ כְּהִלְכוֹת הַפֶּסַח. אֵין
מַפְטִירִין אַחַר הַפֶּסַח אֲפִיקוֹמָן.

רָשָׁע מָה הוּא אוֹמֵר. מָה הָעֲבוֹדָה הַזֹּאת לָכֶם. לָכֶם וְלֹא לוֹ. וּלְפִי
שֶׁהוֹצִיא אֶת עַצְמוֹ מִן הַכְּלָל כָּפַר בְּעִיקָּר. וְאַף אַתָּה הַקְהֵה
אֶת שִׁנָּיו וֶאֱמָר לוֹ בַּעֲבוּר זֶה עָשָׂה יי לִי בְּצֵאתִי מִמִּצְרָיִם. לִי וְלֹא
לוֹ. אִלּוּ הָיָה שָׁם לֹא הָיָה נִגְאָל.

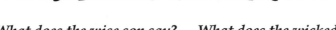

*What does the wise son say? ... What does the wicked
son say? ... What does the simple son say? ... To the
son who does not know what to ask ...*

The wise son is taught the law regarding the Pesach sacrifice,
while the others are told *pesukim* of the Torah. Why does the *Baal
Haggadah* offer this reply for the wise son? The question is even more
puzzling because the wise son's question in the Torah (*Devarim* 6:20)
is followed immediately in the next *pasuk* by the answer, "We were
slaves to Pharaoh in Egypt..." If each type of son has been granted a
level of Torah, what level has been given to the wise son?

How does the *Baal Haggadah* recognize the underlying cynicism of
the wicked son's question, "What does this service mean to you?"
Why does the *Baal Haggadah* instruct us to "blunt his teeth"?

Why does the Torah stress in its answer to the simple son that
Hashem took us out of Egypt with a "strong hand"? Why must the *pasuk* add that we were not only rescued from Egypt, but also "from the
house of bondage"?

Why is the son who does not know how to ask given the same reply as the wicked son, and why doesn't the conclusion of "for me, but
not for him" apply in the case of this son as well?

❀ ❀ ❀

he wise son, what does he say? "What are the testimonies, statutes and the laws that Hashem our G-d, has commanded you?" You should reply to him, (teaching him) laws of Pesach (until their conclusion): One may not eat any dessert after the Paschal sacrifice.

he wicked son, what does he say? "What is this service to you?" (By saying), "to you, but not to himself." Since he has excluded himself from our people at large, he denies the foundation of our faith. Therefore you should blunt out his teeth and tell him: "It is because of this, that Hashem did for me when I went out of Egypt." (By saying) "for me, but not for him." Had he been there, he would not have been redeemed.

· · · ● ❯ ◆━━━━━●·●━━━━━◆ ❰ ● · · ·

Mr. Laufer, an astute businessman, was an excellent judge of character. As his four sons grew older, he assessed their talents and capabilities. He wanted them to be part of his company, but he recognized that each one would have to be given the job that best fit his abilities. After discussing the matter with his partners, Mr. Laufer went ahead and arranged for his children to enter the business.

His eldest son, Shmuel, was a bright young man with logical skills and a sharp mind. Mr. Laufer was pleased to assign him a task involving the manufacture and organization of the company's products. Shmuel threw himself into his job with the greatest enthusiasm, inspecting each product carefully and ensuring that everything ran as smoothly as possible.

תָּם מָה הוּא אוֹמֵר. מַה זֹּאת. וְאָמַרְתָּ אֵלָיו בְּחֹזֶק יָד הוֹצִיאָנוּ יי מִמִּצְרַיִם מִבֵּית עֲבָדִים:

וְשֶׁאֵינוֹ יוֹדֵעַ לִשְׁאוֹל אַתְּ פְּתַח לוֹ. שֶׁנֶּאֱמַר וְהִגַּדְתָּ לְבִנְךָ בַּיּוֹם הַהוּא לֵאמֹר בַּעֲבוּר זֶה עָשָׂה יי לִי בְּצֵאתִי מִמִּצְרָיִם.

• • • • ❯ ━━━━ ━ • ━ ━━ ❮ • • • •

Chaim, on the other hand, was a cynic who sneered at other people's hard work. He had no interest in working at his father's business; in fact, he was actually annoyed to be associated with the company at all. He denigrated other people's work as being unnecessary or wasteful, and did little or nothing in his position in sales. He continued coming to work only because his father insisted on it. Yet, he was willing enough to accept the generous salary that the company offered. Whether or not Chaim wished to admit it, he would have found it difficult to procure a job anywhere else with his limited skills.

David was a good honest worker, but he did not possess a fraction of his father's business acumen. The intricacies of running a successful company were completely beyond him, and even simple transactions left him scratching his head in bewilderment. Nevertheless, he was well suited for the task of supplying office equipment for the company, and he did his job willingly.

Mr. Laufer's youngest son, Yaakov, did not even possess David's limited understanding of the business; he saw only a large complex with people rushing from one building to the next, carrying packages or papers. Mr. Laufer realized that Yaakov could never take an active part in the company. Instead, he assigned the young man to walk the halls at night, moving throughout the complex in order to keep thieves at bay. It was a mindless job, but Yaakov still received a handsome salary for his work as a watchman.

The four young men had been working for the company for many years when their father died peacefully in his sleep. After the week of mourning, the four Laufer sons, now heirs to their father's part of the

he simple son, what does he say? "What is this?" You should tell him: "With a strong hand, Hashem brought us out from Egypt, from the house of bondage."

he son who does not know how to ask, you must open him up, as the verse states: "You shall tell your son on that day. It is because of this, what Hashem did for me when I went out of Egypt."

business, arranged a meeting with the other partners to discuss the status of the company, their positions in the business, and the distribution of Mr. Laufer's estate.

Shmuel didn't have to think twice. "You all know that I have essentially run the business these last few years," he said. "I know the company like the back of my hand." With a faint smile and a slight shrug, he told the partners, "Don't worry about it. I'm not going anywhere."

"Well, good for you," snorted Chaim. "I'm happy that I don't have to stick around this business any more. This company is based on silly ideas, ridiculous products, and idiotic proposals. I want no part of it!"

"By all means," one of the partners snapped at him. "If you don't want a part of your father's company, you are welcome to leave. Go on! And since we don't want to 'embarrass' you, we'll be especially careful to make sure that you don't have a position in the company or receive any money from the business!"

David listened to the discussion, troubled. "I don't understand," he said meekly. "Why are we having this meeting? Can't I just go back to work?"

Realizing that David couldn't understand the technicalities of transferring the ownership of the business and the many questions involved with running the company, the partners treated him kind-ly. "It's all right," they assured him. "After all, you're Mr. Laufer's son. Don't worry! You'll always have your position here in the business, and your salary, too."

Yaakov sat silently. He had never understood anything about running the company, much less the changes that were involved now. Knowing that he wouldn't comprehend anything they tried to tell him, the partners merely gave him further instructions. "You just keep walking through the halls, Yaakov. Make sure you're there each night to serve as a watchman, and we'll continue to pay you."

The wise son, with his greater potential, is given more than his portion of the Torah; he also receives the law regarding the Pesach sacrifice, the *Torah Sh'Baal Peh*. Because of his greater capabilities, more is expected of him, beyond the *pasuk*, the verse, that is mentioned in the Torah.

The wise son asks, "What are the laws that Hashem, our G-d, commanded?" With his reverent use of Hashem's name and his reference to our G-d, his true interest in the Torah is revealed. The wicked son, on the other hand, makes no reference to Hashem's name, and thus is only expressing his cynical contempt for the laws of Pesach. He wishes only to mock his brothers' service of Hashem. Because of his attitude, we are told to "blunt his teeth" — to show him, by using his own attitude, that he is only hurting himself. His wish to be excluded from the service will be granted by his exclusion from his people; only those that observe the Torah will be redeemed, both physically and spiritually.

The simple son does not ask about the Pesach laws out of cynicism or contempt, but rather out of confusion and a lack of understanding. This son is gently told that even if he does not comprehend, he is still part of *Klal Yisrael* when he obeys Hashem's commands. For this reason, the answer to the simple son emphasizes his inclusion as a Jew.

"With a strong hand" — as the *Baal Haggadah* indicates later, refers to the pestilence; the *Divrei Shmuel* comments that during the pestilence, Hashem demonstrated the difference between Egyptian and Jew by destroying only those animals that were owned by the Egyptians. If an animal was jointly owned by an Egyptian and a Jew, the animal was spared. The Jew is always separate and distinct from the non-Jew, and remembering the plague of pestilence helps to emphasize this to the simple son.

Similarly, the usage of the term *"from the house of bondage"* is to emphasize that the Egyptians afflicted our forefathers because they were Jews. The simple son, too, is part of this, no matter how little he understands of his precious heritage.

The son who does not know how to ask is answered in the same vein as the wicked son, because both sons fail to keep Hashem's laws; but because their intentions are different, the tone of the answers are different. The wicked son defies Hashem's laws, and therefore his teeth are blunted; but the son who does not know how to ask is merely ignorant and not deliberately wicked. Therefore, while the words remain the same, this last son is simply being told that he, too, is a child of Hashem, and was redeemed from the land of Egypt.

יָכוֹל מֵראש חֹדֶשׁ. תַּלְמוּד לוֹמַר בַּיוֹם הַהוּא. אִי בַּיוֹם הַהוּא.
יָכוֹל מִבְּעוֹד יוֹם. תַּלְמוּד לוֹמַר בַּעֲבוּר זֶה. בַּעֲבוּר זֶה לֹא
אָמַרְתִּי אֶלָּא בְּשָׁעָה שֶׁיֵּשׁ מַצָּה וּמָרוֹר מֻנָּחִים לְפָנֶיךָ.

***Does [the obligation to tell the story of Pesach begin]
on the first of Nissan? ... When matzah and maror are
placed before you.***

Why would one think that there is an obligation to begin relating
the redemption from the first of Nissan, two weeks before the *Yom Tov*
of Pesach begins? And why does the *Baal Haggadah* choose to raise the
question at this particular point?

❀ ❀ ❀

Moshe was miserably aware that he had earned a nickname
that he could not shake off. Each day, when he rose,
groaning, from his bed, he felt sure that he would ac-
complish something worthwhile; but as soon as he threw on his
clothes and stumbled out of his house, he headed straight to the
nearest tavern. There, he would order cup after cup of whiskey until he drank himself into a stupor. Thoroughly drunk, he would
somehow stagger home to sleep off the whiskey until the following
day, when the cycle would begin all over again.

Was there any reason to wonder why he was known as "Moshe the
shikkur"?

How he hated that name! The children ran after him, laughing,
when they saw him lurching through the streets; the adults of the city
used his name as a byword and a curse. Moshe longed to reform, to
abstain from drinking and lead a sober life; but somehow, the call of
the tavern was beyond his capability to resist.

One day, Moshe found himself dragged out of the depths of slum-
ber by the insistent banging on the door of his little house. Groaning,
rubbing at reddened eyes, Moshe stumbled to the door and wrenched
it open, ready to shout at the children who disturbed his sleep. His

oes (the obligation to tell the story of Pesach begin) on the first of Nissan? The Torah teaches: "(You shall tell your son on that day," [*i.e., the day of the exodus*]*. From the phrase "on that day," one might infer "while it is still day." (Hence,) the Torah adds "it is because of this." ("This" is the symbols of redemption we can actually see.) Thus [the obligation begins] when matzah and maror are placed before you.*

mouth dropped open in shock when he saw Reb Beinush Osder, the distinguished head of the community, standing by the door.

"May I come in?" Reb Beinush asked politely.

"Of course!" Moshe stammered. "Of course. Yes. Please. Come in, sit down, I'll..." He forced himself to stop babbling and calm down. "Please sit down, Reb Beinush," he managed. "Tell me what brings such an honored guest to my home."

"Moshe," Reb Beinush began, "we need your help."

Moshe blinked. "Me? You need my help? I can't help anyone. And who is 'we'?"

"Actually, you can help, Moshe." Reb Beinush sighed. "And if you don't, the entire community will be lost."

Moshe rubbed his aching forehead, wishing his hangover would go away. "Reb Beinush," he said unhappily, "perhaps you could explain yourself a bit more clearly."

Reb Beinush sat silently for a moment, organizing his thoughts. "Two days ago, a man named John Kaden, a gentile who greatly respects the Jews, came to me in the middle of the night," he said at last. "He warned me that the Jews were in danger. A gang of ruffians, led by a drunkard named Ivan Sulter, is planning a pogrom. They intend to sweep through the city and kill every Jewish man, woman and child in their sight."

Moshe sat back, horrified. "But this is terrible!" he blurted. "Isn't there something that can be done to stop them?"

"We tried, Moshe," Reb Beinush said sadly. "We found this Ivan Sulter in one of the taverns on the outskirts of the city. We plied him with whiskey, we flattered him, we offered him bribes; but nothing seemed to help.

"Then, as he refilled his whiskey glass, he looked at the bottle and began to laugh. He announced that with his great strength, no one could ever out-drink him. But if we could find a Jew who could match him, bottle for bottle, and remain standing even after he collapsed, he would agree to withdraw his gang and leave the people of our city in peace."

Moshe stared at Reb Beinush in disbelief.

"It's outrageous, I know," Reb Beinush agreed. "But it's our only chance, Moshe. Ivan has promised that if we can produce a Jew who can out-drink him, a Jew who can handle his whiskey better than he can, he will cancel his plans for the pogrom. If not..." He shuddered at the prospect.

Moshe stared at the rough wooden surface of the table for several minutes. Then he lifted his eyes to meet Reb Beinush's anxious gaze. "What do you want me to do?" he asked quietly.

Reb Beinush gave a rueful smile. "My dear Moshe, I'm afraid that the entire city is well aware of your proficiency in drinking. You truly are our only hope. No one else, except a few other leaders of the community and yourself, are aware of the situation; we don't dare risk a panic. We'll have to pray that Hashem will grant you the strength to match this ruffian drink for drink and remain standing after he collapses."

He rose from his chair. "Ivan has set a date for two weeks from now," he told Moshe. "As strange as it may sound, I would recommend that you make a point of drinking every day as much as possible, in order to increase your system's tolerance for whiskey. Come, Moshe. You will stay in my house for the time being, so that I can provide you with what you need."

Despite the efforts of the community leaders, word of the incredible contest soon reached the ears of the entire city. The people streamed into the *shuls* to recite Tehillim and beseech Hashem to save them from this terrible threat to their lives. For the first time in his life, Moshe the *shikkur* found himself to be an important personage, as everyone blessed him and wished him the best of success in his upcoming contest against Ivan.

The day of the ominous contest arrived. As the Jews gathered in the *shuls* to ask Hashem to save them in their time of need, Reb Beinush and the other community leaders led Moshe to the tavern just outside the city where Ivan awaited them. Moshe's heart hammered in his chest as he realized that the lives of every Jew in the city depended upon his ability to hold his liquor.

When they entered the tavern, Ivan, a huge bear of a man with a bristling black beard, took one look at Moshe and burst into braying laughter. "This little fellow is going to challenge me?" he roared. "Why, he looks like he'd get dizzy from a single shot of whiskey!" He stopped laughing and glowered at Reb Beinush. "I hope you're not mocking me, for your sake," he said with a hiss. "Remember, if this Jew rolls off his chair before I do, you're all going to die!"

Wordlessly, Moshe sat down at the table across from Ivan. The innkeeper had already set over two dozen bottles on the table, with a single glass in front of each chair. With an air of ceremony, the innkeeper now picked up the first bottle and poured a shot into each glass. Ivan, without taking his gaze off Moshe's pale face, lifted the glass and downed the whiskey in a single gulp. Moshe picked up his own glass, made a *berachah* in a clear, loud voice, and drank.

So it went. Glass for glass, bottle for bottle, the two men matched drinks. Each one swayed in his chair as they picked up their glasses with shaking hands and drank yet another swallow of whiskey. Ivan grew truculent, rumbling threats and slurs as he pounded a fist on the table; Moshe, too, became more belligerent, unabashedly giving the peasant as many insults as he got.

Nearly six hours after the drinking bout had begun, Ivan rose slowly to his feet. He propped himself against the table, staring blearily at Moshe. He tried to lift his glass and take another drink; but then his legs buckled underneath him, and the man slid bonelessly to the floor. Moshe, blinking hard, stared at the fallen man for a moment, then shrugged and drained the contents of his own glass.

The spectators cried out in astonishment and relief. Moshe the *shikkur* had won the contest! The Jews of the city were safe!

מִתְּחִלָּה עוֹבְדֵי עֲבוֹדָה זָרָה הָיוּ אֲבוֹתֵינוּ וְעַכְשָׁיו קֵרְבָנוּ
הַמָּקוֹם לַעֲבוֹדָתוֹ. שֶׁנֶּאֱמַר וַיֹּאמֶר יְהוֹשֻׁעַ אֶל כָּל
הָעָם כֹּה אָמַר יי אֱלֹהֵי יִשְׂרָאֵל בְּעֵבֶר הַנָּהָר יָשְׁבוּ אֲבוֹתֵיכֶם
מֵעוֹלָם תֶּרַח אֲבִי אַבְרָהָם וְאֲבִי נָחוֹר וַיַּעַבְדוּ אֱלֹהִים אֲחֵרִים:

It took several days for Moshe to fully recover, but when he next ventured into the streets, he was acclaimed as a hero. The people made a great celebration in his honor, praising him for his courage in saving the city from a dreadful pogrom. With all the attention and the new respect that he received from all sides, Moshe found it easy to stay away from the whiskey bottle. Life had meaning, and there was no need to drown his sorrows in a drunken stupor. Within a few months, Moshe the *shikkur* no longer existed. Instead, Reb Moshe was a man with a steady job, dozens of friends, and the respect of the entire city.

The following year, the people proposed a commemorative feast to celebrate the miracle of their escape from Ivan's deadly pogrom. While many felt that the best day for such a feast would be the anniversary of the drinking contest in the tavern, others suggested that Moshe's two-week training period played just as crucial a part in the miracle. Which day should be chosen for the celebration?

Upon consultation with the rabbinical leaders of the city, the decision was made: the celebration and feast would take place on the date that Ivan had collapsed in a drunken stupor, for it was truly the pinnacle of their salvation.

❖ ❖ ❖

Earlier in the *Haggadah*, it states that, "The more one speaks about the Exodus from Egypt, the more he is praised." It is obvious that there is a definite point of going beyond the letter of the law in this particular *mitzvah*. The preceding passage regarding the four sons also makes it clear that even the son who does not ask must be told the story, which further

n the beginning, our ancestors were worshippers
of idols, but now He has drawn us close to His
service, as it is written, "So Hashem, the G-d
of Israel, says: 'Your ancestors had always lived beyond
the [Euphrates] River — Terach, the father of Abraham
and the father of Nachor — and they served other gods.'

emphasizes the importance of going beyond the minimum
requirement.

We are told that "in the month of Nissan we were redeemed,
and in the month of Nissan we will be redeemed." The Torah
refers to "This month to you" — this month, Nissan, was giv-
en to *Klal Yisrael* as the first month. Because of this reference to
Nissan as the month of redemption, and due to the tendency
to go beyond the actual stipulation of the *mitzvah*, we might infer that we are commanded to celebrate and relate the Exodus
from the first day of Nissan, two weeks before Pesach begins.

In order to clarify exactly when the *mitzvah* is incumbent
upon us, the *Baal Haggadah* links this *mitzvah* with the son who
does not know how to ask, explaining that we are required to
tell him, "*because of this.*" Clearly, we are pointing something
out to him — the *matzah* and the *maror* — and therefore, the
mitzvah of relating the story of the Exodus applies only to the
night of Pesach.

**In the beginning our ancestors were worshippers of
idols ...**

Why does the *Baal Haggadah* mention at this point that *Klal Yisrael's*
origin stems from idol-worshippers? Indeed, why mention it at all?
And what is the significance of elaborating here about all that
Hashem did and gave to our Forefathers?

❀ ❀ ❀

וָאֶקַּח אֶת אֲבִיכֶם אֶת אַבְרָהָם מֵעֵבֶר הַנָּהָר וָאוֹלֵךְ אוֹתוֹ בְּכָל
אֶרֶץ כְּנַעַן וָאַרְבֶּה אֶת זַרְעוֹ וָאֶתֶּן לוֹ אֶת יִצְחָק. וָאֶתֵּן לְיִצְחָק אֶת
יַעֲקֹב וְאֶת עֵשָׂו וָאֶתֵּן לְעֵשָׂו אֶת הַר שֵׂעִיר לָרֶשֶׁת אוֹתוֹ וְיַעֲקֹב
וּבָנָיו יָרְדוּ מִצְרָיִם.

$\bullet\bullet\bullet\bullet\!\!>\!\!\blacksquare\!\!-\!\!-\!\!\bullet\bullet\!\!-\!\!-\!\!\blacksquare\!\!<\!\!\bullet\bullet\bullet\bullet$

Yerachmiel walked aimlessly down the hall, brooding. The
sounds of Torah reverberated from the walls, soaking the
yeshivah building with spirituality, yet Yerachmiel felt himself
separated from it all.

He wished, for the hundredth time, that studying *gemara* was not
such a difficult struggle for him. With his parents' emphasis on sec-
ular education, Yerachmiel could expect little encouragement at
home. He loved studying in a *yeshivah* and had nothing but the
greatest admiration for those who spent their days and nights im-
mersed in the learning of Torah but he sometimes could not help
feeling that it was not the life for him.

Every time he visited his parents, they pressured him to leave the
yeshivah and pursue a college degree. When he returned to the welcoming halls of the *yeshivah*, his relief at escaping to the beauty of the
Torah world would turn to depression when he realized, yet again,
that he just didn't have what it takes to learn full-time. Maybe his parents were right, and he should leave Torah study to those that were
more capable than he was.

Yerachmiel stopped and thrust his hands deep into his pockets.
Yes, he decided sadly, it was time to make a decision. Much as he
loved the beauty and sanctity of *yeshivah* life, he was only wasting his
time here. He would call his parents and tell them that he would reg-
ister for the following semester in the college of their choice.

"Ah, Yerachmiel!" said a warm, friendly voice. "And how are you
doing today?"

The young man looked up, startled, as Rabbi Levi Billman, one of
Yerachmiel's *rebbeim*, came towards him. Reb Levi's face wore a
bright smile, the same beaming expression with which he greeted his

And I took your Patriarch, Abraham, from beyond that river and I led him throughout all the land of Canaan. And I multiplied his descendants and I gave him Isaac. And to Isaac I gave Jacob and Esau. And I gave Mount Seir to Esau as an inheritance for him and Jacob and his children went down to Egypt."

students each day. Yerachmiel's spirits lightened at the sight of his rebbe, then sank as he realized that once he left the *yeshivah,* he probably would never see Reb Levi again.

"Hello, *rebbe,*" Yerachmiel said.

Reb Levi gave him an astute look. "I don't like the way you said that," he observed. "What's wrong?"

"Nothing," Yerachmiel said unconvincingly. "Really."

Reb Levi folded his arms. "Yerachmiel, I'm not moving from here until you tell me what's troubling you."

Yerachmiel's shoulders slumped. He should have known better than to try to fool Reb Levi. "I'm giving up, *rebbe,*" he blurted. "I'm sorry."

Reb Levi's eyebrows shot up at this. "You're giving up?! But why? Yerachmiel..." He stopped and considered for a moment. "This isn't the place for this conversation. Come, Yerachmiel. Let's go sit down outside, where we'll have a bit of privacy."

Reb Levi led the reluctant boy outside to the park bench situated just beyond the entrance to the *yeshivah* building. Once they were seated, Reb Levi turned to his student and said seriously, "Yerachmiel, I don't understand why you feel you have to 'give up.' You've come a long way, you know. You're doing wonderfully, and I, like all your other *rebbeim,* are very proud of your progress."

"Progress," Yerachmiel said bitterly. "One page at a time."

"We all learn one page at a time," Reb Levi reminded him gently.

"*Rebbe,* you know what I mean! Every word of the *gemara* is a struggle for me. How much longer can I manage like this? My parents don't understand why I love it here, and they keep pressuring me to go to college and get a 'real' education instead. I don't have a father who's willing to study and review with me, the way all the other boys do. Really, with my background, what chance do I have of getting any further?"

Reb Levi had listened in silence as Yerachmiel poured out his worries. At last, he stirred and said, "Yerachmiel, I think I'd like to tell you something personal about myself, but I don't want you to mention it to anyone else. It has to remain a secret, just between the two of us."

Intrigued, Yerachmiel readily agreed to this stipulation. He sat back on the bench and listened eagerly to his *rebbe's* words.

"When I was growing up, my family was not religious," Reb Levi began. He smiled at the shocked expression on Yerachmiel's face. "I know, I know — you see me with my beard and black hat, and you think I've been *frum* all my life. But I didn't start out that way. I'd never even heard of Shabbos, much less *mishnayos* and *gemara*, until a Jewish youth group came to my hometown and arranged a Shabbaton. That was the turning point in my life. Once I was introduced to the beauty of *Yiddishkeit*, I wasn't going to be satisfied with anything else.

"But it wasn't easy," Reb Levi continued. "With my lack of background, I was often completely bewildered and lost when I tried to learn. There were many times when I felt ready to abandon the battle and leave it for others who were better equipped, but I didn't give up. It took me many years, Yerachmiel, and an infinite amount of patience, but step by step, I grew more proficient in Torah study. There were times when I clearly felt that Hashem was guiding me." He smiled. "In some ways, my background actually helped; I was so determined to prove that I could succeed, despite the obstacles of overcoming my early upbringing, that I kept working at it long after another person might have admitted failure."

He put a friendly arm on Yerachmiel's shoulder. "With Hashem's help, I have managed to come this far, but a Jew is always seeking to improve. And you know, Yerachmiel, there are many boys who come from good, solid Torah backgrounds, yet have great difficulty fitting into the yeshivah world. Every person faces his own individual challenge, Yerachmiel. It's up to us to determine how to meet it."

Inspired and encouraged by Reb Levi's words, Yerachmiel remained in the *yeshivah* for many years to come. With time and perseverance, he eventually became a great Torah scholar.

The *Baal Haggadah* deliberately mentions *Klal Yisrael's* ignoble beginnings at this crucial point in the story. After recalling how the Jews were enslaved in Egypt and the depths to which they plummeted, a person might become despondent and assume that it is impossible to achieve greatness when one has already descended to such a low level.

To counter this false assumption, the *Baal Haggadah* reminds us that our forefathers were actually descendants of idol-worshippers; they, too, had a background to overcome. Hashem will offer guidance and assistance to those who truly attempt to grow spiritually; our forefathers serve as a prime example of this. Avraham *Avinu* received Hashem's blessings and was inspired to reach levels far beyond our comprehension, despite his upbringing; Yitzchak, who was worthy of being offered as a sacrifice to Hashem, was only granted offspring through Divine assistance. Yaakov descended to Egypt, a Divine requirement accompanied by Hashem's promise of assistance. In each case, the greatness of our *Avos* was elevated by Hashem's Providence.

Their behavior can be contrasted with that of Eisav, who did not make any attempt to improve himself and denied that every event on earth is orchestrated by Divine Providence. He was ultimately given *Har Seir* — material reward in this world — and forfeited the ultimate reward in the World to Come.

By reminding us of Hashem's guiding hand with this passage, the *Baal Haggadah* helps us comprehend that each of the four sons, despite their individual trials and challenges, are granted Heavenly assistance in the pursuit of their goals.

בָּרוּךְ שׁוֹמֵר הַבְטָחָתוֹ לְיִשְׂרָאֵל. בָּרוּךְ הוּא. שֶׁהַקָּדוֹשׁ בָּרוּךְ הוּא חִשַּׁב אֶת הַקֵּץ לַעֲשׂוֹת כְּמָה שֶׁאָמַר לְאַבְרָהָם אָבִינוּ בִּבְרִית בֵּין הַבְּתָרִים. שֶׁנֶּאֱמַר וַיֹּאמֶר לְאַבְרָם יָדֹעַ תֵּדַע כִּי גֵר יִהְיֶה זַרְעֲךָ בְּאֶרֶץ לֹא לָהֶם וַעֲבָדוּם וְעִנּוּ אֹתָם אַרְבַּע מֵאוֹת שָׁנָה: וְגַם אֶת הַגּוֹי אֲשֶׁר יַעֲבֹדוּ דָּן אָנֹכִי וְאַחֲרֵי כֵן יֵצְאוּ בִּרְכֻשׁ גָּדוֹל:

Blessed be He Who keeps His promise to Israel ...

Why does the *Baal Haggadah* choose to praise Hashem at this point for keeping His promises to us? Isn't it obvious that Hashem fulfills His promise?

Nosson was delighted with his new job. He knew he had good qualifications, but it wasn't always easy for a person with no real experience to get a good position. Now, after months of job-hunting, he was hired to head a department in a company which manufactured appliances.

Nosson threw himself into his new task. He still felt somewhat awed that he'd been given such a responsible position; not only was he in charge of inventory, but he was also supposed to get new accounts. It wasn't easy to handle both aspects of the job at once, but Nosson was determined to do his best.

As the months passed, Nosson grew increasingly uneasy. He knew he was doing an excellent job of handling the inventory and determining which models would be most in demand. The people in his division respected him and worked well with him, keeping everything running smoothly. But the new clients! Despite his best efforts, he still hadn't managed to procure new customers. He felt terribly guilty for failing to do part of his job.

When the summons came to report to Mr. Frankel's office, Nosson felt a wave of dread. Mr. Frankel had hired him in the first place. Was he about to fire him now for his inability to acquire new accounts for the company?

lessed be He Who keeps His promise to Israel; blessed be He. That the Holy Blessed One calculated the end of (our slavery) in order to fulfill His pledge that he said to Abraham in the bris bein habesarim, as it is written, "Know with certainty that your descendants will be strangers in a land that is not their own. (The natives) will enslave them and oppress them for four hundred years. But ultimately I will execute judgement upon the nation which they shall serve. Afterwards, they shall leave with great wealth."

As Nosson entered his employer's inner office, Mr. Frankel motioned for him to close the door. "Sit down, Nosson," he said kindly. "Let's talk."

Nosson sat down gingerly on the edge of his chair, wondering whether he was about to be demoted or worse.

"You're doing an excellent job, Nosson," Mr. Frankel began. "You've become a real asset for the company. You do your job efficiently, you run a smooth show, and you've got your entire branch working together as a team."

Nosson tried to smile at the compliments, even as he waited to hear the rest of it.

"However, ..." Mr. Frankel rested his elbows on the desk and pressed his fingertips together. "When you were hired, I made it clear that your job was twofold. You're not only responsible for inventory, Nosson. You're supposed to be bringing in new accounts as well."

"I know," Nosson admitted. "And it's not for lack of trying, Mr. Frankel. I've been doing my best! I just — well, I just haven't managed it yet."

"Nosson, I really am pleased with your work in inventory. If it was up to me, I'd let it go at that." Mr. Frankel shook his head. "But it's not up to me, Nosson. I also have superiors, you know. I've promised them that if you really can't do both aspects of your job, I will find someone else who can."

יַגְבִּיהַ הַכּוֹס וִיכַסֶּה הַמַּצּוֹת וְיֹאמַר:

וְהִיא שֶׁעָמְדָה לַאֲבוֹתֵינוּ וְלָנוּ. שֶׁלֹּא אֶחָד בִּלְבָד עָמַד עָלֵינוּ לְכַלּוֹתֵנוּ. אֶלָּא שֶׁבְּכָל דּוֹר וָדוֹר עוֹמְדִים עָלֵינוּ לְכַלּוֹתֵינוּ. וְהַקָּדוֹשׁ בָּרוּךְ הוּא מַצִּילֵנוּ מִיָּדָם:

At Nosson's stricken look, Mr. Frankel hastened to add, "Now, I didn't call you in here to tell you that you're fired. Don't give up yet! But there has to be some progress in acquiring new accounts." He took a deep breath. "Nosson, I'm giving you two weeks. If you can get ten new clients for the company within two weeks, I'll speak to the ones in charge and convince them that you're worth keeping on the payroll. But if not…" He lifted his hands and shrugged. "If not, Nosson, then I'm afraid I'll have no choice but to dismiss you."

Nosson left the office shaken, but determined. At least he knew that he was doing a good job on the inventory. Now, if only he could find some new accounts, he could keep this job that suited him so well!

Over the course of the next week, Nosson's enthusiasm was matched only by his dedication. He made phone call after phone call, arranging meetings and giving demonstrations. He did everything in his power to create new accounts for the company. But by the end of the week, for all his effort, he'd only managed to secure three new clients.

He reported to Mr. Frankel's office and updated him on the situation.

"I know I still have seven more to go, sir," he said apologetically, "but I'm getting there." He gave his employer a smile of confidence, hiding his own nervousness. "After all, it's three more than I've managed in all the months I'm here! I'm sure I'll have the rest of them by the end of the week."

As the young man left the office, Mr. Frankel stared after him with a thoughtful expression. What a pity it would be if the company would lose such an excellent employee! He was not only a hard worker, but also a man of exemplary character. Yet, if he didn't manage to find another seven clients in a week's time, he would have no choice but to fire him.

Mr. Frankel suddenly leaned forward and picked up the phone. As he began to dial, he nodded to himself and smiled. He had no choice but to keep his promise to his superiors and make sure that Nosson

We cover the matzah, raise the cup and say:

nd this has stood by our ancestors and by us. Not one alone has risen up against us to destroy us. Rather in every generation, they rise against us to annihilate us. The Holy Blessed One, however, saves us from their hand.

brought in ten new accounts; but there was nothing wrong with helping Nosson out a little. He himself would find new clients and credit them to Nosson's name. In this way, he would be able to keep his word and ensure that the promising young man would remain with the company for a long time to come!

❈ ❈ ❈

In the previous section of the *Haggadah*, we declared that even though our forefathers stemmed from idol worshippers, Hashem helped them reach ever-higher spiritual levels. Now, the *Baal Haggadah* expands on this concept, assuring us that we do not need to fear that spiritual deterioration has caused us to become unworthy of Divine assistance. On the contrary! Hashem, Who "keeps His promise to Israel," rescued *Klal Yisrael* from Egypt at a time when they had sunk to the lowest level of impurity. By compressing the four-hundred-year period of exile into two hundred and ten years of harsh slavery, Hashem snatched the people out of Egypt just in time, thus keeping His promise to the *Avos* by enabling the people to be redeemed.

This is the true praise of "He Who keeps His promise" — not only does Hashem ensure that His promises are kept, but He helps us fulfill the conditions as well!

And this has stood by our ancestors and by us...

Why does the *Baal Haggadah* use the expression, "And this?" What message is offered here for future generations?

❈ ❈ ❈

The three boys slung their water canteens over their necks and strode into the forest. It was a perfect day for hiking — sunny and warm, but not oppressively hot. The well-marked trails would take them deep into the heart of the forest, and it would make it easy to find their way out again. After several hours, Baruch, the most adventurous of the three, proposed that they try to explore away from the trail. "I hear water, don't you? Maybe there's a stream or a pond where we could swim a little!"

"Go off the trail?" Avigdor said doubtfully. "How will we find our way back?"

"We could blaze a trail," Peretz suggested. "Then we wouldn't have any trouble getting back to the trail."

"Oh, come on," Baruch challenged. "Don't be so nervous!" His eyes gleamed. "What's the matter? Scared?"

"Of course not," Avigdor sputtered.

"Good." Baruch boldly stepped off the trail and began pushing his way through the branches. "Well, let's go!" he said, looking over his shoulder as he climbed over a fallen log. "Are you coming or not?"

"We're coming, we're coming!" With a last uneasy glance back at the trail, Avigdor and Peretz followed Baruch into the depths of the forest.

They soon grew hot and sweaty as they tried to find their way through the trees, ducking at the branches that slapped against their faces. Baruch tried to lead them towards the tantalizing sound of water, but he couldn't be quite sure of the direction.

"This is ridiculous," Peretz said finally. He stopped in a small clearing and turned in a circle. "We could be wandering in circles for all we know, and it doesn't sound like the water is getting any closer. I say, let's go back."

"I think so, too," Avigdor agreed. He looked around at the trees that surrounded them on all sides and gave a little shiver. "Besides, this place sort of gives me the creeps."

"It sure does!" Peretz wiped at his forehead. "Come on, Baruch. Let's head back to the trail."

"Okay. Uh, sure." Baruch looked around uncertainly. "I think we go that way."

"You think?" Peretz glared at him. "You mean you don't know?"

Baruch flushed. "Well, I've been breaking branches to serve as a trail, but — well — there are an awful lot of broken branches out here." He swallowed hard, then admitted, "I hate to say this, guys, but I think we're lost."

"Oh, great," Peretz moaned, flopping down on the ground. "Now how are we going to get back home?"

A little unnerved by their predicament, Baruch hung his head. "Look, I'm sorry I even suggested it! I guess I was showing off a little, but I didn't plan for this to happen!"

"Okay," Avigdor said, stepping between the two of them and holding up his hands for calm. "It's done. You may have been wrong to suggest going off the trail, Baruch, but we were wrong to agree. We've all made a mistake and now we just have to figure out how to get back home in one piece."

The others agreed to this. Peretz squinted up at the sky and tried to catch a glimpse of the western sun. "Um, it looks like it's close to sunset," he said uneasily. "We'd better get moving."

Under the heavy shade of the trees, the fading light made it even harder to see. It wasn't long before Avigdor tripped over a thick root and fell. He cried out as a sharp pain shot through his knee.

"Avigdor! What happened?" Peretz and Baruch crouched by his side.

"I think I cut myself," he gasped.

The other boys took a look. Blood welled out of the ugly gash on Avigdor's knee.

"Sit still, Avigdor," Peretz urged. He uncapped his canteen and carefully washed the wound. The threesome sighed with relief when they saw that the blood and dirt had made it look much worse than it really was. After several minutes, they finally got the bleeding to stop, but by that time, it was fully dark.

"I don't think we should try making our way through the forest in the dark," Baruch said in a small voice. "Maybe we'd better wait until morning."

"Someone else might get hurt if we try to walk out at night," Peretz agreed anxiously. "But what are we going to do?"

"Let's say some Tehillim, and ask Hashem to help us," Avigdor said.

"Why would He?" Baruch asked miserably. "It's our own fault we're in this mess!"

"That doesn't make any difference," Avigdor retorted. "Hashem will still help us!"

The boys had just completed their eighth chapter of Tehillim when Peretz suddenly gasped and pointed to one side. "Look! Is that a light?"

It was, and the three boys started calling and waving, desperate to catch the attention of whoever was out there. "Maybe they're looking for us," Baruch said hopefully. "Hey! We're over here!"

The light moved closer, and suddenly a man loomed over them, holding a flashlight in one hand and a heavy stick in the other. "What are you doing here?" he growled.

The boys shrank back, frightened. "We got lost," Peretz stammered. "We went hiking and we went off the trail..." His voice trailed off as he saw the man's scowl.

"I'm not going to leave you here where you might be found and report me," he snarled. "Get up, all of you! You're coming with me."

Trembling, the three boys stumbled through the dark night as the man herded them towards a small hut in the heart of the forest. "You'll stay in here," he told them harshly. He shoved them into a tiny room and locked the door behind them. Through the door, they heard him add, "I'll figure out what to do with you in the morning!"

They huddled together in a corner, whispering the words of Tehillim as the tears streamed down their faces and they begged Hashem to rescue them from their plight. What would the man do to them? Would they ever see their parents again?

Hours later, the key turned in the lock and the door opened. They cowered back as a figure stepped into the room, then stopped in astonishment when they saw his uniform. It was a policeman!

"Don't worry, boys," he said softly. "You're safe now."

Peretz, Avigdor, and Baruch ran towards him, almost crying

with relief. "How did you find us?" Peretz asked.

"Your parents got worried when you didn't come home," the officer explained. "We started searching the forest and we found the spot where you went off the trail." As the three boys hung their heads in shame, the policeman continued, "It took us a while, but then we found an area with a lot of mud and fresh human blood, together with some scraps of material — yours, I see," he said, nodding at Avigdor and his torn trousers. "I take it you hurt yourself and washed out the cut? Well, all that water and blood left quite a mess, and it was easy to follow your trail. We found this hut and arrested your 'friend' — he's wanted for robbery, and now we can charge him for kidnapping, too. Don't worry! We'll have him behind bars for quite some time."

He smiled at them. "It's all over, boys. Come. I'll take you home."

The *Baal Haggadah* refers to "this" — the Divine assistance that Hashem granted to Avraham and *Klal Yisrael* in Egypt. The frailty of human comprehension may prevent us from recognizing events as beneficial, but Hashem's guiding hand is actually arranging affairs for our advantage. The horrific oppression of the Egyptian taskmasters seemed an unnecessary cruelty, yet it resulted in an exile of only two hundred and ten years instead of four hundred!

With this passage, the *Baal Haggadah* assures us that all of history, in every generation, is the same. While we might suffer because of our sins, Hashem is always ready to redeem us. Events might seem harsh or cruel, and we might classify disasters as "unfortunate accidents," but Hashem is really guiding the course of our lives to ensure our true salvation!

צֵא וּלְמַד. מַה בִּקֵּשׁ לָבָן הָאֲרַמִּי לַעֲשׂוֹת לְיַעֲקֹב אָבִינוּ שֶׁפַּרְעֹה לֹא
גָזַר אֶלָּא עַל הַזְּכָרִים וְלָבָן בִּקֵּשׁ לַעֲקֹר אֶת הַכֹּל. שֶׁנֶּאֱמַר
אֲרַמִּי אֹבֵד אָבִי וַיֵּרֶד מִצְרַיְמָה וַיָּגָר שָׁם בִּמְתֵי מְעָט וַיְהִי שָׁם לְגוֹי
גָּדוֹל עָצוּם וָרָב: וַיֵּרֶד מִצְרַיְמָה. אָנוּס עַל פִּי הַדִּבּוּר: וַיָּגָר שָׁם. מְלַמֵּד
שֶׁלֹּא יָרַד יַעֲקֹב אָבִינוּ לְהִשְׁתַּקֵּעַ בְּמִצְרַיִם אֶלָּא לָגוּר שָׁם. שֶׁנֶּאֱמַר
וַיֹּאמְרוּ אֶל פַּרְעֹה לָגוּר בָּאָרֶץ בָּאנוּ כִּי אֵין מִרְעֶה לַצֹּאן אֲשֶׁר
לַעֲבָדֶיךָ כִּי כָבֵד הָרָעָב בְּאֶרֶץ כְּנָעַן וְעַתָּה יֵשְׁבוּ נָא עֲבָדֶיךָ בְּאֶרֶץ גֹּשֶׁן:

• • • ▸ ◆ ━━━ • ◆ ━━━ ◆ ◂ • • •

Go out and learn what Lavan attempted to do...

Why does the *Baal Haggadah* mention Lavan's wicked plans in the midst of discussing the atrocities of the slavery in Egypt, and why is it necessary to quote the entire *pasuk* instead of only mentioning that Lavan sought to destroy Yaakov?

❖ ❖ ❖

Peter watched with bitter eyes as the infuriating Jew spoke with the king. It was more than he could bear! Why did the king have to defer to Sir Samuel Geffern like that? Oh, it was true that the man was wealthy, a successful businessman with a very shrewd head on his shoulders. But he was a Jew! A religious Jew! How could the king treat him with such respect?

On many occasions, Peter had taken advantage of his favored position as the king's prime minister to whisper that the Jew was not trustworthy. "All Jews are greedy," he'd warned the king. "All Jews are thieves... All Jews are conniving..." But the king only laughed and brushed Peter's insinuations aside, saying that Sir Samuel had always served him loyally and well.

And now, here Sir Samuel was again, discussing a prospective tax with the king. Peter ground his teeth together. Enough was enough. He was going to rid the kingdom of this parasite, once and for all!

That very night, Peter arranged for a clandestine meeting to

Put down the cups and uncover the middle matzah

o out and learn what Laban the Aramean attempted to do to our father, Jacob. Pharaoh decreed only against the males, but Laban
attempted to uproot everything, as it is written, "An
Aramean sought to destroy my father. He descended to
Egypt and sojourned there with a small number of people.
There, he became a nation, great, powerful and populous."
He descended to Egypt — compelled by [Hashem's] decree
and sojourned there — this teaches that our patriarch, Jacob did not go down to Egypt intending to settle there but
merely to sojourn there, as it says, "And they (Jacob's sons)
told Pharaoh, 'We have come to sojourn in this land, for
there is no pasture for the flocks of your servants since the
famine is severe in the land of Canaan. Now, please, let
your servants dwell in the land of Goshen.'"

take place in the cellar of his home. Half a dozen court officials —
anti-Semites all — gathered in the dark room and listened to Peter's
persuasive tongue explain his plans to destroy Sir Samuel and the
Jews of the kingdom.

"We all know that the Jew will eventually show his true colors and
cause the king great harm," he declared. "All we have to do is hasten
the event and convince the king to be rid of him before it's too late."

"What will we do?" one of the noblemen asked.

Peter explained his plan. First they would begin with small acts of
vandalism, carefully planting evidence that would point to various
Jewish citizens. Then they would present the king with forged docu-
ments to "prove" that Sir Samuel was actually embezzling from the
king's treasury, abusing the trust he had been given. Once a spirit of
suspicion and distrust had been firmly established, it would be easy

to gradually deprive the Jews of their rights. At that point, it would be only a short step to enslaving them, exiling them from the kingdom, or killing them outright.

"It's a long-range plan, and it will take some time," he conceded, "but a slow and steady plot has a much greater chance of success than a wild scheme to destroy all the Jews at once."

The others agreed, but one of courtiers raised an objection. "It does mean that we will be causing damage to the king's property," he said unhappily. "Isn't there some way we can avoid this?"

"It will be much less damage than it would be if Sir Samuel is permitted to continue unchecked," Peter soothed him. He looked around. "Well? Are you with me?"

They nodded silently, and Peter smiled.

"Excellent," he declared. "I will set things in motion. The first act of vandalism will take place next week, and we will all rejoice at the beginning of the Jews' end!"

Two days later, the king summoned Peter for a private audience. "My dear Peter," he said seriously, "I have an important assignment for you. It will be somewhat dangerous, but I know I can trust you to have the kingdom's best interests in mind."

"Certainly, Your Majesty," Peter bowed.

"As you know, we are considering an invasion of Hadel."

Peter nodded. The nearby kingdom was small, but possessed many valuable resources.

"I need you to go to their seaport, the city of Ellerim, and determine the strength of their navy. I think it would be best to attack by sea, but I must know how many ships they have first."

Peter looked thoughtful. "I'd better not go as myself, then. Not as prime minister."

"No, that wouldn't be wise," the king agreed. "It would be best if you simply traveled there as an ordinary citizen, visiting another country. You'll have to be careful, Peter. Relations between our kingdoms are not particularly cordial right now."

"I'll do my best for you, Your Majesty," Peter promised. He gave a fleeting thought to his plans for Sir Samuel and the Jews of the kingdom. He'd have to wait until he came back before he set the plan in motion.

The following morning, Peter departed for the city of Ellerim in Hadel. Obeying the king's instructions, he said nothing of his plans to anyone else, even his closest friends. The six noblemen who were privy to the plan against the Jews assumed that his departure had something to do with their secret plot, but no one dared to breathe a word.

Peter never came back. A formally worded letter, sent by the governor of Ellerim, reached the king nearly two weeks later. The letter explained that a man had been accidentally killed; when they examined the body, they discovered papers that identified him as a citizen of the neighboring kingdom. The governor expressed his regrets and hoped that relations between the two kingdoms would not further deteriorate because of this unhappy incident.

The king sat staring at the letter for a long time. It was easy for him to read between the lines and recognize the veiled warning. Peter had been killed for spying, and the governor was sending a warning that any further attempts would most likely be met by war.

At last, he stirred and spoke to the court. "Gentlemen," he said sadly, "I am sorry to tell you that our beloved prime minister, Peter, has been killed." As the gasps echoed through the great room, he added reluctantly, "the death was… an accident."

To the six men involved in Peter's plan to destroy the Jews of the country, the king's words carried a hidden threat. Peter's plot must have been discovered, and the king had ordered him to be executed! Afraid to even look at each other, the six noblemen silently resolved to drop their plans immediately. It was clear that the king would not tolerate such schemes.

The insidious plot against the Jews was abandoned, and Sir Samuel Geffern and his people never discovered the threat that had loomed over their heads and been averted by a miracle.

Previous passages expounded upon the importance of faith in Hashem's word and His guidance of the world, whether or not we understand how the pieces fit together. Now, the *Baal Haggadah* expands the concept to include incidents of which we are not even aware, yet are still part of Hashem's master

בְּמְתֵי מְעָט כְּמָה שֶׁנֶּאֱמַר בְּשִׁבְעִים נֶפֶשׁ יָרְדוּ אֲבוֹתֶיךָ מִצְרָיְמָה וְעַתָּה שָׂמְךָ יי אֱלֹהֶיךָ כְּכוֹכְבֵי הַשָּׁמַיִם לָרֹב:

וַיְהִי שָׁם לְגוֹי. מְלַמֵּד שֶׁהָיוּ יִשְׂרָאֵל מְצֻיָּנִים שָׁם:

גָּדוֹל עָצוּם. כְּמָה שֶׁנֶּאֱמַר וּבְנֵי יִשְׂרָאֵל פָּרוּ וַיִּשְׁרְצוּ וַיִּרְבּוּ וַיַּעַצְמוּ בִּמְאֹד מְאֹד וַתִּמָּלֵא הָאָרֶץ אֹתָם:

וָרָב כְּמָה שֶׁנֶּאֱמַר רְבָבָה כְּצֶמַח הַשָּׂדֶה נְתַתִּיךְ וַתִּרְבִּי וַתִּגְדְּלִי וַתָּבֹאִי בַּעֲדִי עֲדָיִים שָׁדַיִם נָכֹנוּ וּשְׂעָרֵךְ צִמֵּחַ וְאַתְּ עֵרֹם וְעֶרְיָה: וָאֶעֱבֹר עָלַיִךְ וָאֶרְאֵךְ מִתְבּוֹסֶסֶת בְּדָמָיִךְ וָאֹמַר לָךְ בְּדָמַיִךְ חֲיִי וָאֹמַר לָךְ בְּדָמַיִךְ חֲיִי:

plan. Just as we thank Hashem for the open miracles of Pesach, so too must we express gratitude for His salvation from secret plots that might not ever come to light. Lavan may have tried to destroy Yaakov, but the entire *pasuk* emphasizes that not only did he fail, but Yaakov's descendants eventually left Egypt with a nation that was "great, mighty, and numerous"!

∼∽∼

"And he descended to Egypt" — compelled by Divine decree ... "With a small number of people" — as it says ... "Great and mighty" — as it says..."And numerous" — as it says ... And I said to you, 'Through your blood you will live.'"

Why does the *Baal Haggadah* record the teachings taught on the *pasuk*, and what is the lesson they offer?

❀ ❀ ❀

Reb Chaim Kaufman glanced at his watch and regretfully closed his *gemara*. It was nearly nine o'clock; time to head for home. Tomorrow would be another day in which he could immerse himself in the beauty of Torah study.

ith a small number of people — as it is written, "Your ancestors went down to Egypt with seventy individuals. Now Hashem has made you as numerous as the stars of the sky." There he became a nation — this teaches that Israel became distinct there.

reat, powerful — as it is written, "The children of Israel were fruitful, became prolific, multiplied and became very, very powerful. The land became full with them."

nd populous — as it is written, "I made you as numerous as the plants of the field. You grew and developed, becoming very beautiful, your breasts firm and you hair grown long; but you were naked and bare. I passed over you and saw you weltering in your blood, and I said to you: Through your blood, you will live. And I said to you: Through your blood you will live."

As he walked out of the *beis medrash* where he now spent his days, he couldn't help but smile to himself. It was marvelous to be able to learn full time. For over two decades, as he and Yocheved raised their two sons, Torah study had been a precious commodity, snatched from his busy workday whenever he could spare a few hours. Now that his sons were grown and married with families of their own, Chaim was finally able to spend his time the way he'd always wanted: learning Torah.

Yes, Hashem had truly blessed them. Both of his sons had remained in their hometown, raising beautiful families of their own. Reb Chaim and Yocheved often presided over lively family gatherings — a *simchah*, a *kiddush*, or a *Melave Malka* — and it delighted them to see how wonderfully the grandchildren played together, cousins

וַיָּרֵעוּ אֹתָנוּ הַמִּצְרִים וַיְעַנּוּנוּ וַיִּתְּנוּ עָלֵינוּ עֲבֹדָה קָשָׁה:

וַיָּרֵעוּ אֹתָנוּ הַמִּצְרִים כְּמָה שֶׁנֶּאֱמַר הָבָה נִתְחַכְּמָה לוֹ פֶּן יִרְבֶּה וְהָיָה כִּי תִקְרֶאנָה מִלְחָמָה וְנוֹסַף גַּם הוּא עַל שֹׂנְאֵינוּ וְנִלְחַם בָּנוּ וְעָלָה מִן הָאָרֶץ.

••••❯━━━━━━━━━━━❮••••

and siblings treating each other with friendship and equality.

Yocheved greeted him at the door. He took one look at her face and instantly knew that something was wrong.

"What is it?" he asked quietly as he closed the door behind him.

"Come and eat," she suggested, forcing a smile and avoiding his question. "We'll talk afterwards."

He ate wordlessly as she sat down at the table, speaking aimlessly of safe topics. When he finished his meal, he sat back and looked at her.

"Now," he said, "tell me what's wrong."

"I spoke to Mottel and Shimon today," she began heavily. "The news wasn't good…"

Reb Chaim listened in silence as Yocheved told him what their sons had divulged: both were suffering from a rare, complicated disease. When Shimon received his diagnosis, the doctor had warned him that the illness ran in families. Shimon had suggested that Mottel consult a doctor of his own; sure enough, both brothers had been stricken with the same disease.

"And the prognosis?" Reb Chaim asked, dreading the reply.

"If they get the right treatment, then with Hashem's help, they'll be fine."

Reb Chaim looked up sharply at Yocheved's odd reply. "What do you mean, if they get the right treatment? Why shouldn't they?"

Yocheved sighed. "The only doctor who knows how to deal with this disease doesn't live here." She paused. "They'll have to travel to a different country, Chaim, and they'll have to stay there for months, maybe a year."

"Well," Reb Chaim said slowly, "if that's the only thing to do, then we'll just have to put our faith in Hashem that it all goes well." He stood up. "So, when are we going to leave?"

nd the Egyptians were cruel to us. They made us suffer and imposed harsh slavery upon us. And the Egyptians were cruel to us, as it is written, "Come, let us deal cleverly with them, lest they multiply. Then, if there would be a war, they might join our enemies and drive (us) from the land."

"What?"

Reb Chaim smiled and shrugged. "We're a family, Yocheved. If our boys have to spend months in a foreign country, then it's our job to go along and offer our support."

Word soon spread through the city that the entire Kaufman clan, from the grandparents to the youngest grandchild, were planning to uproot themselves and travel to a distant country. Many protested and urged Reb Chaim and Yocheved to reconsider. "Why take the whole family?" they argued. "You're traveling to a country with no religious Jews, no community, no schooling for the children — it's a spiritual wasteland out there! Let the two men that need the treatment go on their own. You can stay here and care for your grandchildren!"

"We are going to stay together," Yocheved answered, gently but firmly.

When the arguments persisted, Reb Chaim elaborated. "This isn't a frivolous journey or vacation, and we aren't settling in a new country on a whim; we are moving because we have been compelled by a Divine decree, the illness that my two sons have contracted. It is of utmost importance that we stay together and support one another throughout this ordeal!"

Less than three weeks after the doctors had first diagnosed the disease that plagued Shimon and Mottel, the entire extended Kaufman family left their hometown and traveled overseas to their new, temporary lodgings. They knew it wasn't going to be easy; they would have to learn to cope with a new language, a new culture, and an environment that was completely different from anything they'd ever known. Nevertheless, they were determined to make the best of it.

וַיְעַנּוּנוּ. כְּמָה שֶׁנֶּאֱמַר וַיָּשִׂימוּ עָלָיו שָׂרֵי מִסִּים לְמַעַן עַנֹּתוֹ בְּסִבְלֹתָם וַיִּבֶן עָרֵי מִסְכְּנוֹת לְפַרְעֹה אֶת פִּתֹם וְאֶת רַעַמְסֵס:

וַיִּתְּנוּ עָלֵינוּ עֲבֹדָה קָשָׁה. כְּמָה שֶׁנֶּאֱמַר וַיַּעֲבִדוּ מִצְרַיִם אֶת בְּנֵי יִשְׂרָאֵל בְּפָרֶךְ.

The initial adjustment proved very difficult. Their strange attire drew incredulous looks from the local inhabitants, who had never seen a religious Jew before; they had to create their own haven of *Yiddishkeit* without any support from a community network. Consultations with the specialist regarding the onset of treatment only added extra anxiety to the situation.

Reb Chaim and Yocheved took it all in stride. They dealt with curious questions from strangers with friendly politeness, yet maintained a proper distance. Reb Chaim quickly organized the grandchildren, arranging a strict schedule to maintain their *yeshivah* studies. Yocheved supervised the large household, using a mixture of ingenuity and common sense to create a kosher home in the midst of an alien country. Despite the many obstacles that stood in their way, the two of them created a stable home and environment for the family.

The weeks turned into months, then years. Shimon and Mottel continued to undergo a strict medical regimen under the supervision of their specialist; they were also able to procure decent jobs to maintain a livelihood. The Kaufman family, which had grown with the passage of time, became a major influence in the city. Their integrity and honesty earned them the respect of the locals. The Kaufmans were proud that they had made the best of a difficult situation and managed to create a true *kiddush Hashem*.

❀ ❀ ❀

When Yaakov *Avinu* was commanded by Divine decree to go down to Egypt, he understood that the journey would not mean a permanent move, but a temporary one. Despite the discomfort of dwelling among an alien people, Hashem

hey made us suffer, as it is written, "they placed taskmasters over them to oppress them with hard labor. And they built Pisom and Ramses as storage cities for Pharaoh." And imposed harsh slavery upon us, as it is written, "And the Egyptians made the children of Israel do backbreaking labor."

helped Yaakov and his family of seventy multiply and grow to become a great and mighty nation.

The Aramean sought to destroy my father.... The Egyptians were cruel to us ... We cried out to Hashem, the G-d of our fathers, and Hashem heard our voice ... G-d brought us out of Egypt with a mighty hand ...

The Torah states that once the Jews have taken possession of Eretz Yisrael and dwell there, they are required to fulfill the *mitzvah* of *bikkurim*: "You shall take the first of every fruit... and go to the place that Hashem, your G-d, will choose to make His Name rest there..." (*Devarim* 26) Part of the procedure for fulfilling the *mitzvah* of *bikkurim* involved laying the first fruits of the seven *minim* before the *mizbeyach* (altar) and reciting the verses quoted above.

What is the connection between the *mitzvah* of *bikkurim*, bringing the first fruits of Eretz Yisrael to the Beis Hamikdash, and these *pesukim*?

Why did the *Baal Haggadah* choose to include them in the *Haggadah*, and why did he insert them at this particular point?

L ittle Nochum Gylberg, born four years after his only brother Ari, was a delightful child. His gap-toothed grin charmed everyone who met him, and his sunny disposition made him highly popular with the other children on the block. His second-grade

וַנִּצְעַק אֶל יי אֱלֹהֵי אֲבֹתֵינוּ. וַיִּשְׁמַע יי אֶת קֹלֵנוּ וַיַּרְא אֶת עָנְיֵנוּ וְאֶת עֲמָלֵנוּ וְאֶת לַחֲצֵנוּ:

teacher often confided to his parents that he was a favorite among his classmates as well as with the faculty of the school.

On a warm spring evening, shortly before his bedtime, Nochum forgot his parents' strict rules about leaving the front yard. He wandered down the street, turned one corner and then another, and was soon hopelessly lost. As he stood forlornly on the sidewalk, wondering how he was going to get home, a car pulled up to the curb.

"What's wrong, little boy?" the driver asked. "Are you lost?"

"Yes," Nochum whispered. He sniffed. "I want my Mommy!"

"Well, get in the car. I'll take you home."

Nochum hesitated. Hadn't his mother told him something about getting into cars with someone he didn't know? He couldn't remember, and he did want to get back home, so he clambered inside.

"Good boy," the driver smiled as he accelerated away from the curb. "Now, I have to go home first, but then I'll take you right to your mother."

Nochum nodded wearily, then curled up on the back seat. Within minutes, he was fast asleep, blissfully unaware that the man was taking him further and further away from home with every passing moment.

Meanwhile, Eliezer and Miriam Gylberg were growing frantic. Where could Nochum be? When she'd discovered that Nochum was not playing in the yard, Miriam had quickly made the rounds of all the neighbors, asking if her son was playing in their homes. One child remembered seeing Nochum walking down the block, but no one had seen him since.

By nine o'clock, the Gylbergs agreed that it was time to call the police. Nochum was definitely missing.

The police officers were calming and reassuring, but Eliezer could not help but fear the worst. Where was his son? What had happened to him? Who had taken him? Would they ever see him again?

"Try to calm down, sir," one of the officers said to Eliezer. "You're

e cried out to Hashem, the G-d of our fathers — Hashem heard our voice. He saw our suffering, our difficult labor and our distress.

not helping your son like this, and you have your wife and your older son to consider. We'll keep in touch with you and inform you immediately if anything comes up."

Two long agonizing days passed. Eliezer and Miriam spent every minute glued to the phone, reciting Tehillim as they waited for news. If only there was some way to find out what had happened to their little boy!

As they sat in silence by the kitchen table, Miriam suddenly looked up. "Your cousin Moishe is getting married tonight," she said.

"I know," Eliezer said dully.

"I think you should go."

"What?" Eliezer rose from his chair in astonishment. "I can't leave! The phone might ring any minute! I can't, I —"

"Eliezer," Miriam said gently, "we're tearing ourselves to pieces like this. Go to the wedding. Get out of the house for a little while. I'll stay here by the phone, and I'll get in touch with you the instant something happens."

Eliezer hesitated, considering the idea.

"And take Ari with you."

"Ari?" Eliezer blinked in surprise. "It's too long a trip for a sixth grader, wouldn't you say?"

"Eliezer, Ari is working himself into a worse state than you are. He needs the distraction." Miriam swallowed hard, thinking of her little boy. "You both need it, Eliezer. Take him with you and go."

Eliezer reluctantly agreed, realizing that his wife was right. He and Ari were soon dressed in clothing suitable for a wedding. With a snack included for Ari for the long trip to the wedding hall, father and son got into the car and drove off.

"How far is it?" Ari asked curiously as the car entered the expressway.

"About an hour and a half," his father replied. "The hall is just across the state border."

וַנִּצְעַק אֶל יי אֱלֹהֵי אֲבֹתֵינוּ. כְּמָה שֶׁנֶּאֱמַר וַיְהִי בַיָּמִים הָרַבִּים הָהֵם וַיָּמָת מֶלֶךְ מִצְרַיִם וַיֵּאָנְחוּ בְנֵי יִשְׂרָאֵל מִן הָעֲבֹדָה וַיִּזְעָקוּ וַתַּעַל שַׁוְעָתָם אֶל הָאֱלֹהִים מִן הָעֲבֹדָה:

וַיִּשְׁמַע יי אֶת קֹלֵנוּ. כְּמָה שֶׁנֶּאֱמַר וַיִּשְׁמַע אֱלֹהִים אֶת נַאֲקָתָם וַיִּזְכֹּר אֱלֹהִים אֶת בְּרִיתוֹ אֶת אַבְרָהָם אֶת יִצְחָק וְאֶת יַעֲקֹב:

וַיַּרְא אֶת עָנְיֵנוּ. זוֹ פְּרִישׁוּת דֶּרֶךְ אֶרֶץ. כְּמָה שֶׁנֶּאֱמַר וַיַּרְא אֱלֹהִים אֶת בְּנֵי יִשְׂרָאֵל וַיֵּדַע אֱלֹהִים:

וְאֶת עֲמָלֵנוּ. אֵלּוּ הַבָּנִים. כְּמָה שֶׁנֶּאֱמַר כָּל הַבֵּן הַיִּלּוֹד הַיְאֹרָה תַּשְׁלִיכֻהוּ וְכָל הַבַּת תְּחַיּוּן:

וְאֶת לַחֲצֵנוּ. זוֹ הַדְּחַק. כְּמָה שֶׁנֶּאֱמַר וְגַם רָאִיתִי אֶת הַלַּחַץ אֲשֶׁר מִצְרַיִם לֹחֲצִים אֹתָם:

● ● ● ● ▶ ━━◆━━━━━ ● ◆ ━━━━━ ◀ ● ● ● ●

They were over halfway to their destination when the engine choked and groaned.

"Oh, great, that's just what we need," Eliezer muttered.

"What's wrong, Abba?" asked Ari, craning his neck to see the dashboard.

"The car doesn't sound very happy," Eliezer answered dryly. "Let's get off at the next exit and find ourselves a gas station. I want to get the car checked out."

They'd just pulled into a station when the engine sputtered one last time and went dead. "Well, there goes the wedding," Eliezer sighed. "Stay in the car, Ari. I'm going to go talk to the mechanic." He glanced nervously at his watch. "If there is a mechanic at this hour of the day," he added under his breath.

He walked past the gas pumps and entered the garage, where he was relieved to see a man in grimy overalls bent over the opened hood of a truck. "Excuse me, sir," Eliezer called, "are you the mechanic here?"

The man lifted his head. "Yeah, and I should have gone home two hours ago," he grunted. "Whaddaya want?"

"Ah, engine trouble." Eliezer gestured back towards his car. "I'm

e cried out to Hashem, the G-d of our fathers, as it is written, "And after those many days, the king of Egypt died. And the children of Israel groaned because of the work. And when they cried out because of their slavery, their pleas rose up before Hashem." And Hashem heard our voice, as it is written, "Hashem heard our cries and Hashem remembered His covenant with Abraham, Isaac and Jacob." And He saw our suffering — this refers to the disruption of all family life, as it is written, "And Hashem saw the children of Israel and Hashem took note of it." And our difficult labor — this refers to the children, as it is written, "Every boy who is born must be cast into the river, but every girl shall be allowed to live." And our distress — this refers to the oppression [applied by the Egyptians], as it is written, "I have also seen the oppression which the Egyptians are applying to them."

• • • ▶ ◆━━━━ • ◆━ ━◆ ◀ • • • •

on my way to a wedding, and my car just stopped dead."

"Huh." The mechanic shrugged his shoulders and bent back over the pickup truck's engine. "I've got to finish this before I can go and take a look. Might be another twenty minutes, maybe half an hour. Better go buy a sandwich or something while you wait."

"Er, right. Thanks." Shaking his head, Eliezer walked back to the car. "So much for the wedding tonight..."

"What's happening, Abba?" Ari asked, poking his head out of the car window.

"The mechanic is busy. It looks like we're in for a bit of a wait."

"Oh." Ari looked downcast. "Uh, Abba could you please buy a soda or something? I'm kind of thirsty."

Eliezer smiled at his son. "Sure thing, Ari. I don't know if we're going to make it the wedding. The least I can do is buy you a drink. I'll be right back." He retraced his steps and entered the brightly-lit store adjacent to

וַיּוֹצִיאֵנוּ יי מִמִּצְרַיִם בְּיָד חֲזָקָה וּבִזְרֹעַ נְטוּיָה וּבְמֹרָא גָּדֹל וּבְאֹתוֹת וּבְמֹפְתִים:

the gas pumps. Choosing two cans of soda from the refrigerated section, he set them down on the counter and pulled out his wallet.

"Will that be all, sir?" the cashier asked, glancing out the window towards the gas pumps. "Just the drinks?"

"For now, yes," Eliezer replied.

She rang up the soda and handed Eliezer his change. "Glad to see a caring father," she said brightly.

"Excuse me?"

"That's your son, isn't it?" She pointed past the gas pumps, where Ari could be seen with his head poked out of the car window. "There was a man who came through here two nights ago with his little boy and bought himself a drink. I asked if he wanted a soda for his son too, and do you know what he said?" She looked indignant. "He said, 'What son?' The nerve of some people! He was standing there, holding the boy's hand, and he asked such a question! And such a sweet little boy, too!"

Eliezer stared at her for a long moment and felt his heart begin to accelerate. "Two nights ago, you say?"

"That's right," the woman nodded.

"Ah, was this a regular customer? Someone that you know?"

She thought for a moment. "He comes through here every now and then. The mechanic who works here during the day seems to know him pretty well, but he went home a while ago."

"No, he's still in the garage, working on a pickup truck." Eliezer bit his lip, trying to work up enough nerve to ask the crucial question. "What did this little boy look like?"

Her face softened. "Such a nice-looking child," she remembered. "Blond hair, six or seven years old, the cutest smile."

Eliezer held onto the counter for support. "Do you think I could use your phone?" he said shakily. "I have to call the police…"

Forty minutes later, Eliezer borrowed a police officer's portable phone and made another phone call, this time to his own home.

nd *Hashem* brought us out of Egypt with a mighty hand, and with an outstretched arm, and with great visions, and with signs and with wonders.

"Miriam?" he said. "I'm on my way home — and I've got Nochum."

That night, after Nochum had been safely tucked into bed and the house had calmed down again, Eliezer walked into his back yard and looked up at the starry night sky.

"Thank you, Hashem," he whispered. "Thank you for causing the car to break down, for making the mechanic work late tonight, for Ari's presence in the car to prompt the cashier to make that casual comment. Thank you, Hashem, for causing the chain of events that gave me back my son."

❖ ❖ ❖

Agriculture demands a tremendous amount of toil and painstaking labor. When the first fruits ripen, we acknowledge our gratitude to Hashem for giving us this marvelous gift: our inheritance. The *mitzvah* of *bikkurim* includes the recital of verses that acknowledge our appreciation, our *hakaras hatov*, that Hashem has given us the land of Eretz Yisrael. The events leading to our eventual acquisition of Eretz Yisrael were fraught with pain and suffering; but these *pesukim* help us to understand that the difficult times were designed to lead us directly to the good.

This may be one way to define the term *hakaras hatov* — it is not just "recognition of goodness," but recognizing the goodness, the good that is inherent in every situation, even if we might think otherwise. We suffered at Lavan's hands, we descended to Egypt and suffered oppression, but it all ultimately led to Yaakov becoming a "nation, great, mighty, and numerous."

This appreciation of events that lead to ultimate redemption surely has its place in the *Haggadah*!

*The Egyptians did evil to us ... The Egyptians were
cruel to us — as it says (Shemos 1:10) ... And afflicted
us — as the Torah says (1:11) ... And imposed harsh
slavery upon us — as the Torah says ...*

What is the message that the Torah transmits with this passage?

Menachem Stern looked wearily at his only son. Ariel lounged on the couch, a sulky expression on his face. Menachem realized that it would only be counterproductive to continue the discussion.

"All right, Ariel," he sighed. "We'll talk about it another time."

The young man stalked out of the room, his back stiff with outrage. Mr. Stern watched him go, then sat back and sighed. What was he going to do now?

Menachem Stern had amassed a considerable fortune over the years. His honest, yet shrewd business practices had ensured that he would be able to leave his son a comfortable inheritance. Still, it would be unhealthy for Ariel to become a lazy heir who did nothing but spend his days in idleness. Yet how could he convince his son that it would be worthwhile to develop a work ethic, to learn how to manage his own affairs?

Perhaps, he mused, he was going about this the wrong way. Instead of trying to persuade Ariel that he should learn to work hard, he might do better if he offered Ariel an incentive — something that would make him want to work. Even if the boy began with an ulterior motive, he would still be gaining the skills he needed.

Mr. Stern put his new plan into motion the next day. As Ariel sat down to breakfast after the morning prayers, Mr. Stern asked casually, "Tell me, Ariel. Is there anything special that you really like?"

Ariel, ready for another argument about his lack of ambition, blinked in surprise. "Anything special?"

"Yes, Ariel. Is there anything that you really admire, something that you would want to have?"

Ariel stirred his coffee thoughtfully. "I'll tell you," he finally said. "I really love gemstones. I'm always amazed at the beauty Hashem can give to something that's essentially a rock. Diamonds, in particular, are incredible — they're colorless, yet they flash with all the colors of the rainbow."

Mr. Stern tried to hide his surprise at Ariel's sudden eloquence. "Diamonds, eh?" he murmured. "Hmmm. Let me get back to you."

That evening, as Ariel wandered back into the house, Mr. Stern met him at the door. "I have an interesting proposition for you, Ariel," he said briskly. "Come into the study, will you?"

Ariel followed his father warily. "Is this about my going to work?"

"In a way, I suppose so," Mr. Stern conceded. He held up his hand as Ariel opened his mouth to protest. "Now, hear me out. You mentioned diamonds this morning, right?"

"Yes," Ariel said, frowning.

"Well, I made a few inquiries on your behalf today. It seems that a jeweler that I know is planning to retire. He showed me one real beauty of a diamond that he wants to sell. I thought you might be interested."

"Well, sure," Ariel stammered. "But how…?"

"He should be here shortly," Mr. Stern continued. "I told him you'd want to see the diamond before you purchased it."

On cue, the doorbell chimed. Mr. Stern waved a hand at his bewildered son. "Well, go ahead, Ariel," he said briskly. "Answer the door and let him in."

Ariel obediently escorted the elderly jeweler into his father's study. Mr. Stern stood up and shook the man's hand warmly.

"So, this is the young man who likes diamonds, hmm?" the dealer smiled. "Well, take a look at this beauty and tell me what you think."

He produced a small box from his pocket and opened it with a flourish. Ariel gasped with wonder. A superbly cut diamond was nestled inside the box, its many facets refracting the light from the study into dozens of shifting rainbows.

"Worth quite a lot, isn't it?" the elderly man remarked. He handed Ariel the box so that the young man could take a better look. "Now, if you're willing to discuss price…"

Ariel listened silently as his father dickered with the aging jeweler. Finally, they agreed upon a price.

"And the time limit?" Mr. Stern asked.

The jeweler shrugged. "If your boy doesn't take it, Menachem, I've got that offer from Katz. I'm willing to hold onto it for a couple of months — half a year, say, or maybe a bit more — but after that, I'd like to have all the business behind me."

"Fair enough." Mr. Stern shook the man's hand again. "We'll be in touch with you."

The man retrieved the diamond from Ariel and smiled at him warmly. "Best of luck, my boy," he said. "I hope to do business with you."

Mr. Stern escorted the man to the door, leaving Ariel standing almost in a trance. After a moment, Ariel shook off his reverie and hurried after his father.

Mr. Stern had just finished closing the front door when Ariel rushed up to him. "Do you really mean it?" he asked excitedly. "Are you really going to buy that diamond for me?"

Mr. Stern looked at him calmly. "Of course not, Ariel."

Ariel couldn't believe his ears. "But you —"

"Ariel, come back into my study and we'll talk."

In the privacy of the study, Mr. Stern turned to his son decisively. "Ariel, I don't deal in jewels. You told me that this is what interests you. Well, I found you a dealer, I found you a gemstone, and I got you a good price. The rest is up to you, Ariel. If you can earn the money in the next few months, that diamond is yours."

"Earn it?" Ariel asked incredulously. "I can't make that much money!"

"I don't see why not," said Mr. Stern. "You live here, and I supply you with room and board. It's not as if you'll have to support yourself. Get yourself a job, Ariel. Earn enough cash, and you'll be able to buy the diamond."

Even after Mr. Stern left the room, Ariel remained frozen in place, staring out the window. A vision of the magnificent diamond shimmered before his eyes. Could he really manage to earn enough to own that beautiful gemstone?

He slowly nodded his head. "I can," he said softly. "At least, I'm going to try."

It took several days before Ariel managed to find a job; his skills were mediocre at best. Nevertheless, Ariel threw himself into his new profession, learning the tricks of the trade and growing more experienced with the passage of time. His employers, noting his enthusiasm, encouraged him by allowing him to move on to more sophisticated tasks that paid a better salary. Ariel continued to work hard, long hours, counting the pennies until he would earn enough to purchase that lovely diamond.

As the weeks slowly turned into months, Mr. Stern began to feel concerned. Ariel had, indeed, changed from a lazy young man to a hard industrious worker. But if he didn't manage to earn enough to buy the diamond, his disappointment would surely destroy his motivation. Yet Mr. Stern knew that at the rate Ariel was earning, he would not make enough to pay for the diamond. What could be done to ensure the success of Ariel's venture?

He called Ariel's employers and explained the situation. They soon agreed upon a plan that would be for Ariel's benefit, despite the appearances.

The following morning, when Ariel arrived at work, he was surprised to see his employer waiting for him with a scowl on his face. "We're stepping up the pace, Ariel," the man said abruptly. "We expect more work from you — we want you working harder, and for longer hours. Business won't wait for slackers. Either accept the longer hours, or find yourself another job!"

Ariel felt somewhat hurt by this sudden change of attitude, but he was unwilling to do or say anything that might get him fired. He merely nodded his head meekly and went to his workstation.

His employers continued to pressure him, demanding that he work longer and harder than ever before. Ariel returned home each evening, utterly drained and exhausted. The only thing that kept him going was the knowledge that his increased production meant an increased salary.

Mr. Stern observed the situation carefully. He was pleased to see the numbers growing in Ariel's savings account. It was close, very close... but not close enough. The dealer called him to warn him that Ariel had only two months left in which to close the deal. Mr. Stern realized with a touch of dismay that this time, the situation really demanded drastic measures.

Once again, he arranged a meeting with Ariel's employers. This time, they were reluctant to acquiesce. "He's doing so well," they protested. "Do you want us to crush the spirit out of him completely?"

"It's for his own good," Mr. Stern assured them, even as he winced at what his son would have to handle. He withdrew a fat wad of bills and placed them on the table. "Use this if you need it to supplement his salary, but for his own sake, make sure he makes his deadline!"

Ariel was summoned to the main office the following morning. "Ariel, you're a good worker, but we need more," the manager told him. "We've got a major order coming in, and we've got to do everything we can to make the deadline. From now on, I want you here at 7:00 a.m. You'll eat lunch and supper here at work, too, and I don't want you leaving the building before 9:00 at night. It'll be tough, I know, but this is what we need. I think you'll be up to it."

The next two months were sheer torture for Ariel. He worked frantically, knowing that if his pace slackened, he would be summarily dismissed. The payment for his long hours of overtime was very generous, but Ariel was not sure he could survive the grueling schedule.

Just two days before the jeweler's deadline, Ariel knocked on his father's door. "I did it," he whispered. "I've made enough money to buy the diamond."

Mr. Stern hugged his son. "That's marvelous, Ariel," he said, his voice thick with emotion. "You worked incredibly hard to get it done in time, but you did it. Come along, my son. Let's go right now and pick up your precious stone."

❖ ❖ ❖

Hashem told Avraham *Avinu* that the Jews would suffer exile in Egypt for four hundred long years. In His great mercy, Hashem caused that time to be compressed to a period of two hundred and ten years; the terrible suffering that the sadistic Egyptians caused the Jews in that short period of time was the equivalent of four hundred years of regular slavery. While the affliction and hard labor may have seemed evil in the eyes of the Jews, in truth, it was really for their benefit.

We cried out to Hashem, the G-d of our fathers (De-varim 26:7) — as the Torah says ... and their shouts rose up to Hashem because of the work.

Why does the Torah specify that Hashem not only heard the cry of the Jews in Egypt, but also saw their privation, toil, and distress?

Mr. Thraller pressed a button and called, "Send in the next appointment, please."

"Yes, sir," replied the disembodied voice of his secretary.

Mr. Thraller took advantage of the next few moments to try and arrange his paperwork into some semblance of order. The vice-president of one of the biggest banks in the city rarely had time to get properly organized.

He had just finished sorting through his latest reports when the door opened tentatively. A religious woman entered the room, her face pale and her eyes red.

"May I help you?" asked Mr. Thraller. "Please, sit down."

"Thank you," the woman replied hoarsely. She perched at the edge of a chair, twisting her fingers together.

Mr. Thraller studied her carefully. For some reason, she looked familiar.

"My name is Mrs. Sarah Pfiffer," the woman began.

Mr. Thraller blinked. Pfiffer! Of course. He'd heard the rumors. This was the poor woman that —

"You may have heard about me," she continued, her voice weak and tired. "My family was attacked three days ago. Ruffians burst into our home in broad daylight." She swallowed hard. "I tried to scream for help, but..." She lowered her head. "They knocked me out. When I finally woke up again, I found the house torn to pieces, our valuables gone, and — and my husband and children missing."

She started crying quietly. Mr. Thraller sat and waited patiently, his heart aching with sympathy for this woman's suffering, until she managed to compose herself.

"I've discovered that they threw my husband into the labor camp just outside the city, but my two sons — there's been no word. We have no idea where they are." She held up her empty hands. "We are helpless, Mr. Thraller. My family and I need someone of influence — someone like you — to have the criminals brought to justice and my husband and children restored to freedom." The tears began to trickle down her face again. "Please, please, can't you help us?"

"I assure you, Mrs. Pfiffer, that I will do all I can to assist you," Mr. Thraller said quietly. "But with your permission, I would like to come see your home. If I could personally see the scene of the crime, I believe I can be much more effective."

Mrs. Pfiffer was somewhat puzzled by the request, but she readily agreed. Mr. Thraller escorted her out of his office and followed her directions to her desolate home.

Mr. Thraller stepped inside and gasped aloud with shock. The house was in utter shambles. Furniture lay overturned, every windowpane was smashed, broken dishes littered the floor, and clothing, torn and shredded, lay strewn about the house. The three small children who had not been snatched by the ruffians lay huddled in one corner of the room, whimpering to themselves.

For several long moments, Mr. Thraller merely stood there, his expression betraying his horror at the appalling situation. Then he turned to the hapless woman, his face filled with determination. "Leave everything to me, Mrs. Pfiffer," he declared. "With Hashem's help, we will solve all your problems as soon as possible!"

Before Mrs. Pfiffer could utter a word, Mr. Thraller literally ran out of the house. She stared after him, wondering what even a man of his means and influence could do to ease her situation.

The answer was not long in coming. Within an hour, people began streaming into the house, bringing fresh clothing, food, and eager hands to straighten the mess. Mrs. Pfiffer watched with disbelieving eyes as her house was transformed from a forlorn crime scene to the warm, comfortable home that it had been before the attack. And that night, just as her children were preparing for bed, Mr. Thraller appeared — with Mr. Pfiffer and the two missing boys!

The joyful reunion was enough to bring tears to even the most jaded of hearts. As Mr. Thraller stood by, smiling at the happy scene, the Pfiffers stumbled over themselves in their efforts to thank him for all he had accomplished on their behalf.

"I was glad to help," he demurred. "It was the least I could do."

Still, the family remained profoundly grateful to the man who had done so much to save them from their horrific situation. A strong friendship sprung up between Mr. Pfiffer and Mr. Thraller, and they often spent time together.

"Tell me," Mr. Pfiffer asked one day, "why did you ask my wife to let you see the house before you began to pull the strings to arrange for my release? Surely you believed her story?"

"Of course I did," Mr. Thraller replied. He reached down and picked up his own small son, hugging him tightly. "But by personally witnessing your tragedy, I was motivated to do so much more. When I heard your wife describe your plight, I was deeply moved; but when I saw, with my own eyes, how your family was suffering, I was ready to do anything I possibly could to help."

Hashem, in His great mercy, heard the cries of the Jews. But Hashem, as it were, wished to raise those tears to an ever greater, more personal level. Therefore, "He saw our privation" — Hashem saw how the Egyptians attempted to break up their family life, which is a main objective of Hashem in this world; "our toil," which refers to the sons that Pharaoh sought to murder; and "our distress," which refers to the great suffering that the Egyptians imposed on the Jews.

וַיּוֹצִיאֵנוּ יי מִמִּצְרַיִם. לֹא עַל יְדֵי מַלְאָךְ וְלֹא עַל יְדֵי שָׂרָף וְלֹא
עַל יְדֵי שָׁלִיחַ. אֶלָּא הַקָּדוֹשׁ בָּרוּךְ הוּא בִּכְבוֹדוֹ
וּבְעַצְמוֹ. שֶׁנֶּאֱמַר וְעָבַרְתִּי בְאֶרֶץ מִצְרַיִם בַּלַּיְלָה הַזֶּה וְהִכֵּיתִי כָל
בְּכוֹר בְּאֶרֶץ מִצְרַיִם. מֵאָדָם וְעַד בְּהֵמָה וּבְכָל אֱלֹהֵי מִצְרַיִם
אֶעֱשֶׂה שְׁפָטִים אֲנִי יי: וְעָבַרְתִּי בְאֶרֶץ מִצְרַיִם בַּלַּיְלָה הַזֶּה אֲנִי וְלֹא
שָׂרָף. וּבְכָל אֱלֹהֵי מִצְרַיִם אֶעֱשֶׂה שְׁפָטִים. אֲנִי הוּא וְלֹא הַשָּׁלִיחַ.
אֲנִי יי הוּא וְלֹא אַחֵר:

בְּיָד חֲזָקָה. זוֹ הַדֶּבֶר. כְּמָה שֶׁנֶּאֱמַר הִנֵּה יַד יי הוֹיָה בְּמִקְנְךָ
אֲשֶׁר בַּשָּׂדֶה בַּסּוּסִים בַּחֲמוֹרִים בַּגְּמַלִּים בַּבָּקָר וּבַצֹּאן דֶּבֶר
כָּבֵד מְאֹד:

Hashem brought us out of Egypt ...
"Hashem took us out" — not through an angel...
"With a mighty hand" — this refers to the pestilence...
"With an outstretched arm" — this is the sword...
"With great fearfulness" — this refers to the Divine
Presence...
"With signs" — this refers to the staff...
"With wonders" — this refers to the blood...

Why does the *Baal Hagaddah* stress that it was Hashem alone who
carried out the redemption of *Klal Yisrael,* and what is the significance
of the references that lay within the *pasuk*?

❀ ❀ ❀

George Ambiyalo had served his country for close to thirty
years. He'd risen through the ranks of the army until he
earned the rank of general, and now he was acknowledged as
the undisputed head of the armed forces. His soldiers admired him,
not only for his brilliant grasp of tactics and his unquestionable
courage, but also for his high moral standards.

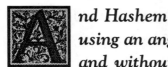nd Hashem brought us out of Egypt — *without using an angel, and without using an archangel, and without using a seraph and without using any agent. Rather [it was] the Holy Blessed One Himself in His glory, as it is written, "And I will pass through the land of Egypt on that night and I will slay every firstborn in the land of Egypt, from man until beast. I will execute judgements against all the gods of Egypt. I am Hashem." And on that night I will pass through the land of Egypt — I and not an angel; and I will slay every firstborn — I and not an archangel; and I will execute judgements against all the gods of Egypt — I and not an agent; I am Hashem — it is I and none other.*

ith a mighty hand — this refers to the Plagues, as it is written, "Behold, the hand of Hashem will be against your cattle in the field, against the horses, the donkeys, the camels, the oxen and the sheep, with a very severe plague."

Ambiyalo was, perhaps more than anything else, a shrewd judge of character. Over the years, he had managed to develop a loyal, well-knit group of officers who carried out his orders implicitly. With mutual respect and a high degree of self-confidence, his officers led the army units to war under Ambiyalo's direction, following his inspired tactics to ultimate victory.

Other countries, aware of General Ambiyalo's reputation, preferred to avoid attacking a land that was so well protected by its army. For the most part, Ambiyalo and his officers led the soldiers in peacetime drills, encouraging them to keep up their training. It was a time to build strength, a time to encourage the soldiers to think for themselves

וּבִזְרֹעַ נְטוּיָה. זוֹ הַחֶרֶב. כְּמָה שֶׁנֶּאֱמַר וְחַרְבּוֹ שְׁלוּפָה בְּיָדוֹ נְטוּיָה עַל יְרוּשָׁלָיִם.

וּבְמֹרָא גָּדֹל. זוֹ גִּלּוּי שְׁכִינָה. כְּמָה שֶׁנֶּאֱמַר אוֹ הֲנִסָּה אֱלֹהִים לָבוֹא לָקַחַת לוֹ גוֹי מִקֶּרֶב גּוֹי בְּמַסֹּת בְּאֹתֹת וּבְמוֹפְתִים וּבְמִלְחָמָה וּבְיָד חֲזָקָה וּבִזְרוֹעַ נְטוּיָה וּבְמוֹרָאִים גְּדֹלִים כְּכֹל אֲשֶׁר עָשָׂה לָכֶם יי אֱלֹהֵיכֶם בְּמִצְרַיִם לְעֵינֶיךָ:

━━━━━━━━━━━━━━━━━

instead of blindly following orders. Ambiyalo was pleased that his "boys" were learning the importance of morality, of judging the enemy, and differentiating between their opponents in war and innocent bystanders.

Then the unthinkable happened. The situation had been steadily deteriorating for a number of months, but now the neighboring country declared outright war. Ambiyalo and his army were going to have to fight, and this time, things weren't going to be so simple.

General Ambiyalo summoned his loyal officers to an emergency meeting. They all knew Ambiyalo well, and one look at his face told them that the matter was even more serious than the prospect of war.

"Gentlemen," he said gravely, "the first battles will begin within the next few days. We all know that we're going to go out there and do the best we can for our country. But this time, we can't just take our soldiers out and order them to start shooting. We are facing a challenge unlike anything we've ever dealt with before."

He swiveled around and pointed at the map on the wall. "As you all know, the borders have been in dispute for some time now. Unfortunately, several communities, villages that are unquestionably part of our country, have been absorbed by the enemy. We have gotten reports that many of the civilians have been forcibly pressed into service — some as slaves, and some as conscripts to their army."

An appalled silence settled over the room as the officers absorbed the awful implications. The enemy wouldn't hesitate to place the forced conscripts on the front lines of the battle. This meant that

ith an outstretched arm — this refers to the sword, as it is written, "His drawn sword is in His hand, stretched out over Jerusalem."

 ith great fear — this is the revelation of the Divine Presence, as it is written, "Has Hashem ever performed miracles, coming to take a nation from the midst of another with miracles, signs, wonders, war, a mighty hand and an outstretched arm, and with terrifying events, as Hashem did for you in Egypt before your eyes?"

when they went to war, they would essentially be killing their own people!

"Under these circumstances," Ambiyalo continued, "there is going to be a change of plans. I want you all to understand that this doesn't reflect a lack of confidence in your abilities —" He took a deep breath. "But I'm going to lead the army myself. I'm going to the front this time."

The officers reacted with murmurs of astonishment. Ambiyalo's declaration went against every rule of warfare. The top leaders never risked their lives and indispensable abilities at the forefront of war, but rather remained safely behind the lines, receiving constant reports and directing the battle. How could General Ambiyalo risk himself in such a fashion?

"I will not condone the senseless killing of our own people," Ambiyalo said quietly. "This conflict is not a regular war, gentlemen. The very people we are sworn to protect are going to be forced into the ranks of the enemy. The situation calls for delicacy. Someone of ultimate authority is going to have to be right on the spot to differentiate between the enemy soldiers who want to fight us and the forced conscripts who want nothing more than to live in peace. And that person, gentlemen, is going to be me."

No one argued with Ambiyalo. His reasoning was flawless. Who

וּבְאֹתוֹת. זֶה הַמַּטֶּה כְּמָה שֶׁנֶּאֱמַר וְאֶת הַמַּטֶּה הַזֶּה תִּקַּח
בְּיָדְךָ אֲשֶׁר תַּעֲשֶׂה בּוֹ אֶת הָאֹתֹת:
וּבְמֹפְתִים. זֶה הַדָּם כְּמָה שֶׁנֶּאֱמַר וְנָתַתִּי מוֹפְתִים בַּשָּׁמַיִם
וּבָאָרֶץ.

• • • • > ━━ ━ • ━ ━━ < • • • •

wanted to shoulder the responsibility of making such decisions? Only
the general himself could handle such a situation.

"One more thing," Ambiyalo added. "Our enemy has been aggressive for too long. Part of our task is to intimidate them to the point
where we're not going to have to worry about any other attacks in the
future. I'm not talking about whole-scale killing, but a show of intelligence, endurance and clear superiority. Once the enemy realizes
what they're up against, I suspect that they'll retreat and never both-
er us again."

The plan was soon set in motion. The soldiers marched proudly,
awed to see General Ambiyalo himself leading them into war. The
men were ordered to avoid bloodshed at all costs, capturing the enemy instead of killing them. The ultimate decision of who would be
killed and who would be permitted to live would remain in Ambiyalo's hands alone.

With lightning strikes, the army advanced, capturing key positions
and ambushing the enemy when they least expected it. Ambiyalo
carefully ordered the execution of the enemy officers, leaving the
common soldiers to retreat in fear and confusion. Those soldiers who
were clearly forced conscripts were taken into protective custody and
eventually granted their freedom.

Word of Ambiyalo's brilliant strategies spread through the enemy
ranks, undermining their confidence and security in their own fighting abilities. The man seemed to be everywhere, directing the battle
with exquisite precision. Soon, even the mere mention of his name
was enough to leave the enemy soldiers cowering in fear.

When Ambiyalo saw that his tactics were working, he ordered one
last attack in order to leave a permanent mark on the enemy. With an

nd with signs — this refers to the staff, as it is written, "Take this staff in your hand, with which you will perform the signs."

 nd wonders — This refers to the blood, as it is written, "I will reveal wonders in heaven and earth."

open display of the most modern equipment, Ambiyalo's army efficiently destroyed the most strategic and crucial areas in the enemy's territory. Very little life was lost, but the demoralized enemy was forced to concede that there was nothing it could do to stop the brilliant general from attacking at will. Less than twenty-four hours later, the enemy retreated in disorganized defeat. Ambiyalo was the undisputed victor of the war!

❀ ❀ ❀

Hashem, in His great mercy, executed the redemption from Egypt Himself. It was "not through an angel" or any other intermediary who would fail to differentiate between Egyptian and Jew at the time of punishment. The blood that the Jews brushed onto the door posts was required only as an act of pure faith, for Hashem Himself conducted the redemption and had no trouble determining each person's status.

Some of the commentaries apply this explanation to the plague of pestilence, in which the Torah states, "The hand of Hashem is on your livestock... And Hashem shall distinguish between the livestock of Yisrael and Egypt." (*Shemos* 9:3,4) Hashem spared the cattle of the Jews with exquisite precision, to the point where an animal that was jointly owned by a Jew and an Egyptian was also not stricken with the pestilence. This is the "mighty hand" of Hashem, a Divine Revelation of His power that was met "with great fearfulness"; and the "signs and wonders" were designed to leave a permanent, everlasting impression of Hashem's great might.

≈≈≈

שׁוֹפְכִים מִן הַכּוֹס לְכָל אַחַת שָׁלשׁ פְּעָמִים לְשָׁלשׁ דְּבָרִים הַלָּלוּ

דָּם וָאֵשׁ וְתִמְרוֹת עָשָׁן:

דָּבָר אַחֵר. בְּיָד חֲזָקָה שְׁתַּיִם. וּבִזְרֹעַ נְטוּיָה שְׁתַּיִם. וּבְמֹרָא גָּדֹל שְׁתַּיִם. וּבְאֹתוֹת שְׁתַּיִם. וּבְמֹפְתִים שְׁתַּיִם. אֵלּוּ עֶשֶׂר מַכּוֹת שֶׁהֵבִיא הַקָּדוֹשׁ בָּרוּךְ הוּא עַל הַמִּצְרִים בְּמִצְרַיִם. וְאֵלּוּ הֵן:

Another interpretation: "With a mighty hand" ...

Why did the *Baal Hagaddah* include "Another interpretation" which
has an allusion to the Ten Plagues that struck Egypt?

❈ ❈ ❈

Rabbi Hilstein sighed quietly to himself as Aryeh strolled inso-
lently into the classroom. This was nothing new; Aryeh rou-
tinely arrived at least ten minutes late, and never seemed the
slightest bit apologetic for disturbing his classmates. It all fit with the
rest of the boy's attitude. Aryeh was rude, belligerent, and arrogant.
Not only did he clearly feel that he was superior to his classmates —
and Rabbi Hilstein himself — but he translated his temperament into
insults, sneers and sometimes even physical retaliation when one of
his peers dared to contradict him.

Repeated attempts at talking to Aryeh's parents had shown Rabbi
Hilstein exactly why the boy behaved in such a fashion. Aryeh's parents spoiled him terribly, showering him with gifts and indulging his
every demand without ever giving him any kind of discipline for his
misbehavior. His contempt for others was fostered by his parents' de-
plorable habit of voicing their disapproval of others, including
Aryeh's teachers, in front of their son. Aryeh absorbed their opinions
and attitudes, and grew to consider himself an authority on every
subject that affected his life.

To the other boys in the class, Aryeh was nothing more than a
mean-tempered bully; but to Rabbi Hilstein, the young man was a
child that was desperately crying for help. Determined to somehow
reach Aryeh and teach him proper *middos*, Rabbi Hilstein spent hours

One pours out three drops of wine; one for each word

Blood, Fire, and Columns of Smoke.

nother interpretation: *With a mighty hand: two; with an outstretched arm: two; with great visions: two; with signs: two; and with wonders: two. These are the ten plagues which the Holy Blessed One brought upon the Egyptians in Egypt. And they are:*

thinking of the best way to show the boy how he should act.

Rabbi Hilstein finally arrived at a decision. Aryeh behaved the way he did because he simply did not know any better. He needed to be taught, but how? He'd experienced indulgence from his parents, and attempts at punishing him had only failed in the past. It wouldn't be easy, but the only way to reach Aryeh was through a combination of methods: strict discipline when the situation required it, and friendly encouragement to act as positive reinforcement.

"With Hashem's help, I will manage," he said aloud. He consulted other educators, discussed the situation with the principal, and set his plan into motion.

The following morning, when Aryeh entered the room, Rabbi Hilstein did not ignore his tardiness. "Aryeh, class begins at eight o'clock, not at eight fifteen," he said sharply. "Make sure you get here on time."

Aryeh looked at his *rebbe* with shock that quickly mutated into anger. With a sullen expression, he turned away and slouched to his place, banging his notebooks on the desk and scraping his chair loudly on the floor.

"A little more quietly, Aryeh," Rabbi Hilstein reminded him. "You've disturbed the class already. Don't make it worse."

Aryeh sulked for the rest of the morning, but as the boys filed out of the room for lunch, Rabbi Hilstein made a point of speaking to him. "You know, Aryeh, that was an excellent question you asked in *gemara* yesterday. Keep up the good work."

שׁוֹפְכִים מִן הַכּוֹס בְּכָל תֵּיבָה

דָּם. צְפַרְדֵּעַ. כִּנִּים. עָרוֹב. דֶּבֶר. שְׁחִין.
בָּרָד. אַרְבֶּה. חֹשֶׁךְ. מַכַּת בְּכוֹרוֹת:

Aryeh stopped short and frowned at Rabbi Hilstein. Without a word, he turned and followed the other boys to the lunchroom, but Rabbi Hilstein felt sure that the young man had appreciated the compliment.

The following morning, Aryeh was actually in class on time. Rabbi Hilstein, secretly delighted, maintained a calm and friendly expression as he commended the boy for his promptness. Aryeh said nothing, but quietly opened his notebook and prepared for class.

A few days later, Rabbi Hilstein spotted Aryeh having an argument with one of his classmates. He strode forward just in time to hear Aryeh deliver a particularly vicious insult.

"That's quite enough, Aryeh!" Rabbi Hilstein said sharply. "I will not tolerate that kind of language in this classroom!"

Aryeh turned red with anger and tried to argue with his *rebbe*, but Rabbi Hilstein held firm. "You are a *yeshivah* boy and you will behave like one. Is that clear?"

Aryeh glared at Rabbi Hilstein, then turned and stomped away. Before the day was over, Rabbi Hilstein made sure to find a reason to compliment Aryeh. The boy, still sulking from the earlier reprimand, accepted the words of praise reluctantly; nevertheless, Rabbi Hilstein saw Aryeh's face soften. Was it really working?

The days turned slowly into weeks. Rabbi Hilstein called upon his deepest stores of patience in dealing with Aryeh. He refused to allow the boy to step over the line, but he made sure to encourage him at the same time. He expanded the project to include the other boys in the class, treating them all with the same firm discipline and smiling encouragement. There were days when Rabbi Hilstein went home in despair and other times when he felt exhausted beyond endurance, but he persevered. Slowly but surely, the difference in the classroom became apparent. The boys were maturing, developing the necessary discipline for proper behavior.

One pours out ten drops of wine; one for each plague

Blood; Frogs; Lice; Wild Beasts; Cattle Plague; Boils; Hail; Locusts; Darkness; Slaying of the Firstborn.

At the end of the year, Rabbi Hilstein made a party for his students. In his parting speech, he observed that they'd all grown tremendously over the year. "I will miss all of you," he told them, "but I have given you one very important gift that you will use for the rest of your lives: discipline. You have all matured a great deal this year, and I'm proud of how far you've all come."

After the party ended, the boys came forward one by one to thank their *rebbe* personally. Aryeh hung back until the others had left the room, then stepped forward shyly. "*Rebbe*," he said hesitantly, "I have to admit there were times when I didn't understand what you were doing to me. I don't think I fully understand it now. But there's one thing I know for sure, and that's that you did it all to help me."

Rabbi Hilstein, deeply moved, took Aryeh's hand. "It was all for your own good, Aryeh," he said softly. "I had your best interests in mind. You've matured beautifully, and I'm proud of you."

Aryeh nodded. "I know you did, *Rebbe*. I felt it. And… thank you."

❂ ❂ ❂

When Hashem redeemed the Jews from Egypt, He exacted punishment, measure for measure, for the suffering that the Egyptians inflicted on the Jewish people:

Blood — to remind the Egyptians of the innocent blood that they spilled.

Frogs — in retaliation for the creeping animals that the Egyptians forced the Jews to collect.

Lice — because the Egyptians forced the Jews to sweep the dust from the streets, the dust turned into lice.

Wild Beasts — the Egyptians sent the Jews to hunt wild animals at the risk of their lives, so they were plagued by wild animals.

שׁוֹפְכִים מִן הַכּוֹס שָׁלֹשׁ פְּעָמִים בַּאֲמִירַת שְׁלֹשֶׁת סִימָנִים

רַבִּי יְהוּדָה הָיָה נוֹתֵן בָּהֶם סִמָּנִים: דְּצַ"ךְ. עֲדַ"שׁ. בְּאַחַ"ב.

מוֹזְגִים הַיַּיִן לִמְלֹאוֹת הַכּוֹסוֹת

Pestilence — since they ordered the Jews to herd their cattle, the cattle died.

Boils — the Egyptians had humiliated the Jews by forcing them to prepare their baths; the boils made it impossible for the Egyptians to bathe.

Hailstones — to punish the Egyptians for forcing the Jews to become stonecutters.

Locusts — since the Egyptians made the Jews labor in the fields, all of their produce was consumed by the locusts.

Darkness—the Egyptians imprisoned the Jews and denied them freedom of movement, so the darkness held them immobile.

Slaying of the First Born — because the Egyptians murdered the Jews, who Hashem calls His first born, the first born of the Egyptians were killed.

The concept of measure for measure was designed not only to punish the Egyptians, but also to instruct and elevate the Jews in their understanding. The plagues themselves played a major part in the redemption, for it helped the Jews see Hashem's greatness in His exact judgment. For this reason, the *pasuk* refers to the plagues as part of the redemption of the Jews as well as a punishment for the Egyptians.

❧❧❧

Rabbi Yehudah coined abbreviations for them: Detzach, Adash, B'Achav

Why did Rabbi Yehudah find it necessary to group the plagues together in this fashion?

❀ ❀ ❀

Pour out a drop of wine for each of the three words

Rabbi Yehudah coined abbreviations for them:

Detzach. Adash. B'achav.

The cups are refilled

• • • ❯ ◆━━━━━◆ • ◆━━━━◆ ❮ • • • •

Meir's parents recognized that their son needed something more than the regular school routine. While he did well in all his subjects and was well liked by his teachers and peers, Meir seemed restless. He had a creative mind, and he needed some kind of outlet for his imagination. His parents tried various activities, but nothing seemed to help — until his mother bought him a paint set.

From the moment Meir first picked up a paintbrush, he was hooked. He sat for hours at a time, painstakingly creating pictures and designs. His parents, recognizing their son's talent, encouraged him.

"It's a healthy hobby, after all," his mother smiled. "I'll arrange from some art lessons — just the basics to get him started. If he's still interested after that, we'll take it from there."

Meir devoured his lessons and asked for more. As he learned new techniques and concepts, his paintings became more and more professional. His room slowly transformed itself into a studio as he continued to practice and improve. He scrupulously maintained his regular learning schedule and studied hard for his classes in school, but every spare moment was devoted to painting.

With time, Meir branched into more theoretical studies. One particular subject interested him immensely: the science of colors, the way they were grouped and how they blended and contrasted with each other. He felt fascinated by the way the different colors could be mixed to create new shades and hues. He continued to hone his knowledge, gaining further insight into the exquisite precision with which Hashem had ordered the world of color. What an incredible universe Hashem had created! Every time he learned something new, Meir felt that he had gained a deeper understanding of Hashem's greatness.

❀ ❀ ❀

רַבִּי יוֹסֵי הַגְּלִילִי אוֹמֵר. מִנַּיִן אַתָּה אוֹמֵר שֶׁלָּקוּ הַמִּצְרִים בְּמִצְרַיִם עֶשֶׂר מַכּוֹת וְעַל הַיָּם לָקוּ חֲמִשִּׁים מַכּוֹת. בְּמִצְרַיִם מַה הוּא אוֹמֵר. וַיֹּאמְרוּ הַחַרְטֻמִּים אֶל פַּרְעֹה אֶצְבַּע אֱלֹהִים הִיא. וְעַל הַיָּם מַה הוּא אוֹמֵר. וַיַּרְא יִשְׂרָאֵל אֶת הַיָּד הַגְּדוֹלָה אֲשֶׁר עָשָׂה יי בְּמִצְרַיִם וַיִּירְאוּ הָעָם אֶת יי וַיַּאֲמִינוּ בַּיי וּבְמֹשֶׁה עַבְדּוֹ: כַּמָּה לָקוּ בְּאֶצְבַּע עֶשֶׂר מַכּוֹת. אֱמוֹר מֵעַתָּה בְּמִצְרַיִם לָקוּ עֶשֶׂר מַכּוֹת וְעַל הַיָּם לָקוּ חֲמִשִּׁים מַכּוֹת:

The previous passages of the *Haggadah* expounded upon the exactness with which Hashem punished the Egyptians, paying them measure for measure for the suffering they inflicted on the Jews. Now, Rabbi Yehudah takes that same concept and develops it further, teaching us that there is even more depth to the profundity of the Ten Plagues. By grouping them in this fashion, R' Yehudah alludes to further, greater lessons, as expounded by the various commentaries.

≈≈≈

Rabbi Yosi the Galilean declared: Ten plagues in Egypt and fifty at the sea...
Rabbi Eliezer said: Forty plagues in Egypt and two hundred at the sea...
Rabbi Akiva said: Fifty plagues in Egypt and two hundred fifty at the sea...

What significance lies in the dispute of the Sages? What new appreciation can we gain from such a determination?

Salevia reeled under the attack of its enemies. Town after town fell under the onslaught of the enemy. Some cities were razed to the ground, the citizens tortured and killed; other cities saw all the inhabitants taken prisoner, forced into labor camps and slavery. Where was King Verdelow, and what was he doing to stop the wholesale

abbi Yossi the Galilean declared: What is the source which teaches that the Egyptians were struck by ten plagues in Egypt and were struck by fifty plagues at the [Red Sea]? Concerning the plagues of Egypt, the Torah states, "And the magicians told Pharaoh, 'It is the finger of Hashem.' " With regard to those at sea, the Torah states, "Israel saw the great hand which Hashem wielded against the Egyptians, and the people feared Hashem. They believed in Hashem and in Moses, His servant." With how many plagues were they struck by the finger? Ten. Thus It follows that they were struck by ten plagues in Egypt and fifty at the sea.

slaughter? Where was the king who they had once imagined could protect them from their enemies?

King Verdelow agonized over every setback, wept over each life that was lost. But he knew that his army wasn't ready to fight against the superior enemy. The initial invasion had been so unexpected that the soldiers were woefully unprepared for battle. They fought valiantly, doing the best they could, but his army was constantly driven back, deeper into the heart of Salevia.

The country's morale was at an all-time low when the tide finally turned. Verdelow, personally leading the army, made a lightning attack and managed to drive the enemy away from one of the major Salevian cities. News of the victory raced through the country, bringing sudden hope in its wake. The army, heartened by the unexpected success, continued to train fiercely, following King Verdelow's lead as he devised new strategies and tactics for their battles. Perhaps they would be able to drive the enemy away from Salevia and breathe peacefully once again!

In battle after battle, Verdelow led his suddenly confident army to victory. The country buzzed with the news of the king's fierce prowess and incredible brilliance in war. Awed, the people spoke

רַבִּי אֱלִיעֶזֶר אוֹמֵר. מִנַּיִן שֶׁכָּל מַכָּה וּמַכָּה שֶׁהֵבִיא הַקָּדוֹשׁ בָּרוּךְ הוּא עַל הַמִּצְרִים בְּמִצְרַיִם הָיְתָה שֶׁל אַרְבַּע מַכּוֹת. שֶׁנֶּאֱמַר יְשַׁלַּח בָּם חֲרוֹן אַפּוֹ עֶבְרָה וָזַעַם וְצָרָה מִשְׁלַחַת מַלְאֲכֵי רָעִים. עֶבְרָה אַחַת. וָזַעַם שְׁתַּיִם. וְצָרָה שָׁלֹשׁ. מִשְׁלַחַת מַלְאֲכֵי רָעִים אַרְבַּע. אֱמוֹר מֵעַתָּה בְּמִצְרַיִם לָקוּ אַרְבָּעִים מַכּוֹת וְעַל הַיָּם לָקוּ מָאתַיִם מַכּוֹת:

רַבִּי עֲקִיבָא אוֹמֵר. מִנַּיִן שֶׁכָּל מַכָּה וּמַכָּה שֶׁהֵבִיא הַקָּדוֹשׁ בָּרוּךְ הוּא עַל הַמִּצְרִים בְּמִצְרַיִם הָיְתָה שֶׁל חָמֵשׁ מַכּוֹת. שֶׁנֶּאֱמַר יְשַׁלַּח בָּם חֲרוֹן אַפּוֹ עֶבְרָה וָזַעַם וְצָרָה מִשְׁלַחַת מַלְאֲכֵי רָעִים. חֲרוֹן אַפּוֹ אַחַת. עֶבְרָה שְׁתַּיִם. וָזַעַם שָׁלֹשׁ. וְצָרָה אַרְבַּע. מִשְׁלַחַת מַלְאֲכֵי רָעִים חָמֵשׁ. אֱמוֹר מֵעַתָּה בְּמִצְרַיִם לָקוּ חֲמִשִּׁים מַכּוֹת וְעַל הַיָּם לָקוּ חֲמִשִּׁים וּמָאתַיִם מַכּוֹת:

with admiration for their king's intelligence, his courage, and his power. They'd lost faith for a short while, but now, every citizen of Salevia felt sure that their king was the greatest that had ever lived!

In an effort to truly appreciate their king, a group of experts began to analyze King Verdelow's battle plans, examining every nuance and movement in order to understand the greatness of the man who had brought them their victory. In this way, the people could gain a deeper appreciation of their king and understand how much he truly deserved their praise.

❁ ❁ ❁

The *Baal Haggadah* mentions the dispute of the *Tana'im* to increase our awe and appreciation of Hashem's greatness. A closer analysis of the plagues, and the measure-for-measure punishment that the Egyptians received, serves as another level of inspiration and appreciation of the wondrous mira-

abbi Eliezer said: What is the source [which teaches] that each and every plague that the Holy Blessed One brought upon the Egyptians consisted of four plagues? As it is written, "He unleashed upon them His burning anger, wrath, and fury, and trouble and troops of messengers of evil." "Wrath" refers to one plague; "fury" refers to a second; "trouble" refers to a third; and "troops of messengers of evil" refers to a fourth. Thus we may conclude that they [the Egyptians] were struck by forty plagues in Egypt and they were struck by two hundred plagues at the sea.

abbi Akiva said: What is the source which teaches that each plague that the Holy Blessed One wrought against the Egyptians consisted of five plagues? As it is written, "He unleashed upon them His burning anger: wrath, and fury, and trouble and the troops of messengers of evil." "His burning anger" refers to one plague; "wrath" refers to a second plague; "fury" refers to a third plague; "trouble" refers to a fourth plague; and "messengers of evil" refers to a fifth plague. Thus, we may conclude that they [the Egyptians] were struck by fifty plagues in Egypt and by two hundred and fifty plagues at the sea.

cles that Hashem performed for our sake when He took us out of Egypt.

כַּמָּה מַעֲלוֹת טוֹבוֹת לַמָּקוֹם עָלֵינוּ:

אִלוּ הוֹצִיאָנוּ מִמִּצְרַיִם וְלֹא עָשָׂה בָהֶם שְׁפָטִים   דַּיֵּנוּ:

אִלּוּ עָשָׂה בָהֶם שְׁפָטִים וְלֹא עָשָׂה בֵאלֹהֵיהֶם   דַּיֵּנוּ:

אִלּוּ עָשָׂה בֵאלֹהֵיהֶם וְלֹא הָרַג אֶת בְּכוֹרֵיהֶם   דַּיֵּנוּ:

אִלּוּ הָרַג אֶת בְּכוֹרֵיהֶם וְלֹא נָתַן לָנוּ אֶת מָמוֹנָם   דַּיֵּנוּ:

אִלּוּ נָתַן לָנוּ אֶת מָמוֹנָם וְלֹא קָרַע לָנוּ אֶת הַיָּם   דַּיֵּנוּ:

אִלּוּ קָרַע לָנוּ אֶת הַיָּם וְלֹא הֶעֱבִירָנוּ בְּתוֹכוֹ בֶּחָרָבָה   דַּיֵּנוּ:

אִלּוּ הֶעֱבִירָנוּ בְּתוֹכוֹ בֶּחָרָבָה וְלֹא שִׁקַּע צָרֵינוּ בְּתוֹכוֹ   דַּיֵּנוּ:

אִלּוּ שִׁקַּע צָרֵינוּ בְּתוֹכוֹ וְלֹא סִפֵּק צָרְכֵּנוּ בַּמִּדְבָּר אַרְבָּעִים שָׁנָה   דַּיֵּנוּ:

אִלּוּ סִפֵּק צָרְכֵּנוּ בַּמִּדְבָּר אַרְבָּעִים שָׁנָה וְלֹא הֶאֱכִילָנוּ אֶת הַמָּן   דַּיֵּנוּ:

אִלּוּ הֶאֱכִילָנוּ אֶת הַמָּן וְלֹא נָתַן לָנוּ אֶת הַשַּׁבָּת   דַּיֵּנוּ:

אִלּוּ נָתַן לָנוּ אֶת הַשַּׁבָּת וְלֹא קֵרְבָנוּ לִפְנֵי הַר סִינַי   דַּיֵּנוּ;

אִלּוּ קֵרְבָנוּ לִפְנֵי הַר סִינַי וְלֹא נָתַן לָנוּ אֶת הַתּוֹרָה   דַּיֵּנוּ:

אִלּוּ נָתַן לָנוּ אֶת הַתּוֹרָה וְלֹא הִכְנִיסָנוּ לְאֶרֶץ יִשְׂרָאֵל   דַּיֵּנוּ:

אִלּוּ הִכְנִיסָנוּ לְאֶרֶץ יִשְׂרָאֵל וְלֹא בָנָה לָנוּ אֶת בֵּית הַבְּחִירָה   דַּיֵּנוּ:

How many favors has Hashem granted us!
If He had brought us out of Egypt but had not execut-
ed judgment upon them, it would have sufficed for us...

Why did the *Baal Haggadah* structure the setup of expressing our appreciation through *Dayeinu* — "it would have sufficed us"?

❁ ❁ ❁

Shimon Shapiro sat on the edge of the comfortable chair, shifting nervously under Rabbi Cohen's kind gaze. He could hardly bring himself to look his old *rebbe* in the eye. He knew that something had to be done about his son, Eli, but what?

"Shimon," Rabbi Cohen said gently, "I know you and your wife wait-

ow many favors has Hashem granted us!

If He had brought us out of Egypt but did not execute judgements upon [the Egyptians,] it would have sufficed us.

If He had executed judgements against [the Egyptians], but not against their gods, it would have sufficed us.

If He had executed judgements against their gods but did not slay their firstborn, it would have sufficed us.

If He had slain their firstborn but did not give us their wealth it would have sufficed us.

If He had given us their wealth but did not split the sea for us, it would have sufficed us.

If He had split the sea for us but did not lead us through on dry land, it would have sufficed us.

If He had led us through on dry land but did not drown our foes in it, it would have sufficed us.

If He had drowned our foes in it but did not provide for our needs in the dessert for forty years, it would have sufficed us.

If He had provided for our needs in the desert for forty years but did not feed us the Manna, it would have sufficed us.

If He had fed us the Manna but did not give us the Sabbath, it would have sufficed us.

If He had given us the Sabbath but did not bring us to Mount Sinai, it would have sufficed us.

If He had brought us to Mount Sinai but did not give us the Torah, it would have sufficed us.

If He had given us the Torah but had not brought us into Eretz Yisrael, it would have sufficed us.

If He had brought us into Eretz Yisrael but did not build the Temple for us, it would have sufficed us.

עַל אַחַת כַּמָּה וְכַמָּה טוֹבָה כְפוּלָה וּמְכֻפֶּלֶת לַמָּקוֹם עָלֵינוּ. שֶׁהוֹצִיאָנוּ מִמִּצְרַיִם. וְעָשָׂה בָהֶם שְׁפָטִים. וְעָשָׂה בֵאלֹהֵיהֶם. וְהָרַג אֶת בְּכוֹרֵיהֶם. וְנָתַן לָנוּ אֶת מָמוֹנָם. וְקָרַע לָנוּ אֶת הַיָּם. וְהֶעֱבִירָנוּ בְתוֹכוֹ בֶּחָרָבָה. וְשִׁקַּע צָרֵינוּ בְּתוֹכוֹ. וְסִפֵּק צָרְכֵּנוּ בַּמִּדְבָּר אַרְבָּעִים שָׁנָה. וְהֶאֱכִילָנוּ אֶת הַמָּן. וְנָתַן לָנוּ אֶת הַשַּׁבָּת. וְקֵרְבָנוּ לִפְנֵי הַר סִינַי. וְנָתַן לָנוּ אֶת הַתּוֹרָה. וְהִכְנִיסָנוּ לְאֶרֶץ יִשְׂרָאֵל. וּבָנָה לָנוּ אֶת בֵּית הַבְּחִירָה לְכַפֵּר עַל כָּל עֲוֹנוֹתֵינוּ:

* * * ❯ ◆━━◆ ◆ ◆━━━◆ ❮ * * *

ed a long time before you were blessed with your son. Eli is a bright, intelligent boy. You and your wife must surely thank Hashem every day."

Mr. Shapiro swallowed. "It's true, Rabbi Cohen, and we're grateful, of course. It's just that lately, we've had a problem with Eli. He's — well, Eli doesn't seem to appreciate everything we've done for him. He's — he's..."

"He's a bit arrogant?" Rabbi Cohen suggested mildly. "Automatically expects you to give him whatever he wants? Never bothers with a 'please' or a 'thank you'? Doesn't appreciate everything you and your wife do for him?"

Mr. Shapiro rubbed his forehead. "I'm afraid so," he admitted. "I guess we've spoiled him."

"It's a common enough mistake, Shimon. Even parents who didn't go through the agony of being childless can spoil their children. The problem is catching it before it's too late." Rabbi Cohen leaned forward. "A child who doesn't understand the concept of appreciation, of being grateful for what he has, is stunted. For Eli's own sake, you must teach him that he can't take his blessings for granted."

"How do I do that?" Mr. Shapiro asked.

"You know Eli better than I do," Rabbi Cohen said. "You and your wife should sit down together and discuss the matter thoroughly. I'm sure that with concentration and determination, the two of you will devise a way to teach Eli to appreciate every aspect of what he receives from you."

How much more so [do we owe thanks] to our Hashem for His repeated and manifold favors to us! That He brought us out of Egypt; and He executed judgements against the Egyptians; and He executed judgements against their gods; and He slew their first-born; and He gave us their wealth; and He split the sea for us; and He led us through it on dry land; and He drowned our foes in it; and He provided for our needs in the desert for forty years; and He fed us the Manna; and He gave us the Sabbath; and He brought us before Mount Sinai; and He gave us the Torah; and He brought us into Eretz Yisrael; and He built for us the Temple to atone for all of our sins.

• • • **>** ◆━━━━━◆ • ◆━━━━◆ **<** • • • •

Mr. Shapiro sat quietly in his chair, thinking. After a few minutes, he rose from his chair. "Thank you, Rabbi Cohen," he said gratefully. "I think you're right. Hopefully, we'll figure out a way to make things right."

"May Hashem grant you success," Rabbi Cohen smiled, "and let me know what happens."

Mr. Shapiro returned home and discussed the matter with his wife for hours. The two of them agreed that Eli needed a sharp lesson in appreciation, but what would be the best way to make sure he learned his lesson?

"Talking to him won't help," Mrs. Shapiro pointed out. "We've tried talking to him before."

"You're right," Mr. Shapiro agreed. "He needs to experience it somehow. If we can show him how much he really has, he'll learn to be grateful."

"But how can we do that?" Mrs. Shapiro asked plaintively. "Refuse to give him what he asks? That would only cause arguments, and we're trying to avoid that if we can."

For several minutes, the two of them sat in silence. Then Mrs. Shapiro stirred. "I have an idea," she said, somewhat hesitant, "but it's a little drastic…"

Mr. Shapiro listened to her plan. "You're right that it's a bit extreme," he said thoughtfully, "but if we do it properly, I think it'll do the trick."

That night, Mr. Shapiro called an old friend of his, a man who was an experienced hiker. The two of them discussed the plan in detail and contacted the two people they would need in order to ensure the plan's success. Once everything was finalized, it was up to Eli himself to put the plan into action.

The first step took place the following morning at the breakfast table. As the three of them sat down, Mr. Shapiro remarked casually to his wife, "I was talking to David Lender last night."

"David Lender?" Mrs. Shapiro said. "Oh, isn't he the one who goes hiking all the time?"

Eli, his interest piqued, looked up. "Hiking?"

"That's right," Mr. Shapiro said. "David Lender is an expert. He likes walking the trails in the woods upstate. He always says it's very relaxing."

"Hiking," Eli repeated. "That sounds really neat!"

Mrs. Shapiro looked at him with apparent alarm. "Now, Eli, don't start thinking about doing it yourself. You're too young for that."

Eli's face took on a mulish expression. "I am not too young," he said petulantly. "I'll bet I could hike just as well as Mr. Lender!"

"I don't know," Mr. Shapiro said with an artful frown. "Hiking means roughing it, Eli. You won't find it easy."

"I can do it!" Eli insisted. "I know I can!"

"I'm not sure this is a good idea," Mrs. Shapiro fretted.

"Oh, Ma," Eli groaned. "I'm not a baby! I can do it!"

With some more careful protests from Mrs. Shapiro and some extra hesitation from Mr. Shapiro, the two of them managed to maneuver Eli into agreeing to go camping the following week with David Lender.

"Great," Eli said, rubbing his hands together. "Now, I'll give you a list of what I need for the trip…"

"Just a minute, Eli," Mr. Shapiro interrupted. "If you really want to go hiking, you might as well do it the right way. And that means roughing it. No frills, no luxuries."

Eli hesitated for a moment.

"Are you sure you want to do this?"

Hearing the doubt in his father's voice, Eli set his jaw. "Yes," he declared. "I'll take what Mr. Lender says, and that's all. I know I'll do just fine."

After Eli left for school, the two parents looked at each other.

"Well, that's the first step," Mrs. Shapiro said heavily. "We can trust David Lender, can't we?"

"Absolutely," Mr. Shapiro assured her. "He'll be following Eli every step of the way, you don't have to worry about that."

The week flew by, and school officially ended. Eli was full of excitement as he packed the essentials into his new backpack.

"How come I have to take this boring food along?" he complained.

"A bar or two of chocolate for energy is fine, but you need non-perishables," Mr. Shapiro pointed out. "You can still back out if you want to."

"No," Eli said quickly. "I'm not backing out."

Two days later, Mr. Shapiro drove Eli upstate, where a large forest spread across many acres of wild land. Mr. Lender was waiting for them at the beginning of the trail.

"Good luck, Eli," Mr. Shapiro said, hugging his son. "We'll see you in two days."

Eli looked at the forest, green and dark, and swallowed hard. "Yeah," he said with attempted nonchalance. "See you."

He set off along the trail, with Mr. Lender just ahead. At first, Eli enjoyed the hike. The air under the trees was warm and smelled of life. But as the sun rose overhead, the heat increased and Eli soon grew uncomfortable. He took out his canteen from his backpack, made a *berachah*, and drank. He made a face as he realized the water was warm.

"They could use a soda machine out here," he muttered, knowing perfectly well that it was a ridiculous thought. He tipped back his head and took another hefty swallow.

"Eli, stop!"

"Huh?" Eli looked at Mr. Lender with surprise. "What's wrong?"

"You're drinking too much," Mr. Lender explained. "That one canteen of water has to last you until late this afternoon, when we'll set up camp next to a stream. There's no other source of water before that."

Eli slowly closed the canteen and tucked it back into his backpack. Forget the soda machine! Not even to have as much water as you want? He trudged along, suddenly feeling that hiking wasn't as much fun as he'd thought.

By two o'clock in the afternoon, Eli had had enough. "I need a break," he demanded.

Mr. Lender looked surprised. "But we have to keep going, Eli, or we won't reach the campsite by dark."

"I'm tired!" Eli insisted, his voice rising. "I want to rest!"

Mr. Lender frowned. "We have to continue."

Eli turned and stalked off the trail. He sat down under a tree and leaned against the trunk. "I'm staying here until I feel ready to continue," he declared. "You can go on if you want and set up camp. I'll come when I'm ready."

"Eli, that's dangerous."

"What's the big deal? I'll just follow the trail."

"Well… If you're sure you want to do this?"

"Yes." Eli crossed his arms and closed his eyes.

"All right, then," he heard Mr. Lender say. "But don't wait too long. Make sure you're on your way again within the next half-hour, or you might get lost. I don't want you to be too far behind me."

"I won't get lost," Eli muttered. "I can find my way anywhere!"

Mr. Lender stood for a moment, looking at the rebellious boy. He shook his head in wonder, astonished at the way Mr. Shapiro had predicted Eli's behavior so accurately. Well, it was all part of the plan. Eli would think the older man was far ahead of him, but Mr. Lender would really keep the boy in sight at all times. This was supposed to be a lesson, not actively dangerous.

Some time later, Eli abruptly awakened from a nap he hadn't planned on taking. He sprang to his feet and looked at his watch with dismay. It would be dark in just a few hours! He quickly shouldered his backpack and started along the trail, hoping he would make it to Mr. Lender's campsite before dark.

Some two miles down the trail, Eli stopped short and stared. The trail forked, going in almost opposite directions. Mr. Lender hadn't mentioned this to him! How could he know which way to travel? If he chose the wrong trail, he would be hopelessly lost!

Eli peered down each path, hoping to catch some glimpse of the camping site in the deepening gloom. But the only thing he saw were more trees, and the only things he heard were the rustles of animals moving through the underbrush. He shuddered to himself as he wondered what kind of animals came out at night.

Taking a deep breath, he chose the right fork and started walking.

By the time full night fell, Eli was close to tears. He was sure he'd taken the wrong fork, but he was terrified that if he tried to retrace his steps, he'd miss the turning in the dark. He couldn't see the trail any more, and his flashlight seemed all too feeble against the ominous blackness of the forest. The animal sounds seemed to close in, suddenly much more menacing than they'd been earlier.

With despair, Eli huddled against a tree, wrapping his arms around his knees in a futile effort to keep warm. What was he going to do? His canteen was almost empty and he had no way of finding water. How he wished he'd saved his chocolate bars instead of eating them within the first few hours of the hike! Now he only had tasteless, unappetizing food. Worst of all, he had no shelter. Mr. Lender had carried a large backpack on a frame, complete with a tent, but Eli had nothing but his jacket. How grateful he felt that his mother had insisted that he wear a heavy sweater!

He listened to the sound for almost a minute before he recognized the steady tread as footsteps. He leapt to his feet, unsure if he should call out or try to slip quietly away. Maybe it was Mr. Lender?

"W-who's there?" he called out tremulously.

A sudden beam of light blinded Eli as a man came forward, looking huge and menacing in the darkness. "What's this?" a strange voice asked. "A young boy, alone in the forest at night?"

Eli tried to shield his eyes. "I was going hiking," he stammered, "and I got separated from Mr. Lender."

"Mr. Lender?" the man repeated. "Well, boy, you look like you could use a little help. Not really prepared for a night out in the wild, are you?"

"Not really," Eli admitted.

"Ridiculous, a kid your age out in the forest," the man grumbled. "Why, you could never get back out! No one would even know you were missing."

"That's not true!" Eli protested, tears coming to his eyes. "My parents love me, they care, they'd find me somehow…"

The man shrugged. "Huh. I don't know." He pulled out a canteen. "Need a drink, boy?"

"Yes, thank you," Eli said gratefully. The water was stale, but to Eli, it tasted delicious.

"Well, I can't leave you by yourself," the man said, sounding resigned. "Come along. You'll join me at my campsite tonight. We'll figure out what to do with you in the morning."

Eli followed the man along the trail until they came to a small tent. The man ushered Eli inside. "I've only got a couple of blankets," the man remarked, "so we'll only have one each."

"That's all right," Eli said quickly. "A blanket and a tent is lots better than having nothing at all." He thought wistfully of his soft bed and warm home. How far away it seemed, and how much he'd appreciate his pillow and heavy quilt now!

The man looked at him strangely and smiled to himself. "Well, boy, let's turn in. We'll start out again in the morning."

Eli quickly fell asleep. Once the man was sure the boy was sleeping soundly, he slipped out of the tent and walked several paces away. "David?" he called softly.

Mr. Lender stepped out of the trees. "Is Eli all right?" he asked.

"Just fine," the man replied with a smile. "I'd say another half a day at most is all we'll need. He's well on his way to learning his lesson."

Mr. Lender smiled back. "Good," he said. "I'll be about a hundred feet back if you need help."

"Don't worry, I'll manage," the man assured him. "See you tomorrow afternoon, back in civilization!"

Mr. Lender melted back into the shadows, and the man returned to the tent, wrapped himself in his single blanket, and went to sleep.

The following morning, Eli crawled out of the tent. He stretched his cramped limbs, wishing there were some way he could wash. He looked at his benefactor, who sat on a nearby tree stump, humming to himself. "Sir," he said tentatively, "I really appreciate your help last night, but all I really want to do right now is find a way out of the forest so I can go back home. Can you help me?"

The man looked thoughtful. "I could, but it would take a while," he warned. "A day or two at the least."

"Whatever it takes," Eli said fervently.

The two of them packed the tent and began their journey. This time, Eli didn't complain or demand a break; he trudged along willingly, eager to reach the end of the trail and return to the safety and security of his parents' home. Around noon, they found a stream. Eli took the opportunity to wash, shivering a little as he sluiced icy water over his face. He thought longingly of a hot shower in a heated bathroom, with large, fluffy towels.

"I really miss home," he murmured aloud as he sat on the bank, hoping the sun peeking through the trees would help him dry off.

"Do you, now?" the man asked with a gleam in his eye.

"Oh, yes," Eli said fervently. "If there's one thing I've learned in the past day, it's how much I have. I don't think I'll ever take my parents for granted again!"

"You're just saying that now," the man scoffed. "Sure, it'll feel good to be back in a nice house with everything your parents give you. But what's going to happen when you ask your parents to give you something and they won't? You'll probably be complaining and whining! And I'll bet you don't even appreciate what they do give you."

"That's not true!" Eli protested, without stopping to wonder how this man could know so much about his home. "If I could just get out of here…" He swallowed hard, then continued, "I'd be happy just to be out of the forest. If my parents bring me back home, that would be more than enough. And warm clothing, and food, and sending me to learn and…" He rubbed at his eyes, trying not to cry. "And they help me develop my *middos*, even when I'm not really helping… They do so much for me!"

The man sat back, hiding a smile of satisfaction. "Well, boy, with a list like that, I'd have to agree with you. By mentioning all those items

רַבָּן גַּמְלִיאֵל הָיָה אוֹמֵר. כָּל שֶׁלֹּא אָמַר שְׁלֹשָׁה דְבָרִים אֵלּוּ
בְּפֶסַח לֹא יָצָא יְדֵי חוֹבָתוֹ. וְאֵלּוּ הֵן:

פֶּסַח מַצָּה וּמָרוֹר:

לֹא יֹאחֵז בְּיָדוֹ אֶת הַבָּשָׂר שֶׁהוּא זֵכֶר לְפֶסַח,
שֶׁנִּרְאֶה כְּאִלּוּ הִקְדִּישׁוֹ לְקָרְבַּן פֶּסַח כְּשֶׁאוֹמֵר אֶת זֶה

פֶּסַח שֶׁהָיוּ אֲבוֹתֵינוּ אוֹכְלִים בִּזְמַן שֶׁבֵּית הַמִּקְדָּשׁ הָיָה קַיָּם עַל
שׁוּם מָה. עַל שׁוּם שֶׁפָּסַח הַקָּדוֹשׁ בָּרוּךְ הוּא עַל בָּתֵּי
אֲבוֹתֵינוּ בְּמִצְרָיִם. שֶׁנֶּאֱמַר וַאֲמַרְתֶּם זֶבַח פֶּסַח הוּא לַיי אֲשֶׁר
פָּסַח עַל בָּתֵּי בְנֵי יִשְׂרָאֵל בְּמִצְרַיִם בְּנָגְפּוֹ אֶת מִצְרַיִם וְאֶת בָּתֵּינוּ
הִצִּיל וַיִּקֹּד הָעָם וַיִּשְׁתַּחֲווּ:

one by one, I think you've pretty much proven that you do appreciate everything your parents give you." He stood up and stretched. "Let's get moving. Maybe we'll hit a good trail and manage to get out of the forest before sundown."

The man gestured Eli forward. As the boy walked ahead, the man turned back and waved down the trail. Mr. Lender appeared and waved back, giving his friend a grin. It looked like their mission had been accomplished.

❖ ❖ ❖

Hashem performed incredible miracles for the Jews when He took them out of Egypt. By enumerating each miracle individually instead of lumping them together, we can properly express our appreciation for Hashem's great kindness.

Rabban Gamliel would say ... The Pesach sacrifice: for what reason? ... This matzah that we eat: for what reason? ... This maror that we eat: for what reason? ...

After the recital of *Dayeinu* and the enumeration of the many acts of kindness' that Hashem has done for us, what is the significance of

abban Gamliel would say: Whoever does not discuss the following three things on Pesach has
not fulfilled his obligation. They are:

Pesach [The Passover Sacrifice]
Matzah [The Unleavened Bread]
And Maror [The Bitter Herbs]

We do not lift the shankbone, so as not to appear as if we are
bringing the Korban Pesach, while reciting

he Paschal sacrifice that our ancestors would eat
during the times of the Temple — what is the
reason? Because the Holy Blessed One passed
over the houses of our ancestors in Egypt, as it is written,
"You shall say, 'It is a Pesach sacrifice for Hashem because He passed over the houses of the children of Israel in
Egypt, striking the Egyptians and saving our homes.' The
people bowed down and prostrated themselves."

Rabban Gamliel's teaching? Why is it so important to verbally mention Pesach, *matzah* and *maror*, to the point where one who does not
has not fulfilled his obligation?

❊ ❊ ❊

octor Herman was not just a physician; he was doctor, nurse,
father and friend, all in one. His patients knew he would
care for them as if they were his own children. His thriving
practice was a clear indication of his tremendous popularity.

As the years passed, Doctor Herman began to concentrate his practice on critically ill patients — the ones who needed him most. He
joined the staff of a prestigious hospital and devoted himself to the
chronically ill who desperately needed a caring considerate doctor to
help them endure their sicknesses.

צריך להגביה את המצה להראותה למסובין כדי שתתחבב המצוה עליהם כשאומר את זה

מַצָּה זוֹ שֶׁאָנוּ אוֹכְלִים עַל שׁוּם מָה. עַל שׁוּם שֶׁלֹּא הִסְפִּיק בְּצֵקָם שֶׁל אֲבוֹתֵינוּ לְהַחֲמִיץ עַד שֶׁנִּגְלָה עֲלֵיהֶם מֶלֶךְ מַלְכֵי הַמְּלָכִים הַקָּדוֹשׁ בָּרוּךְ הוּא וּגְאָלָם. שֶׁנֶּאֱמַר וַיֹּאפוּ אֶת הַבָּצֵק אֲשֶׁר הוֹצִיאוּ מִמִּצְרַיִם עֻגֹת מַצּוֹת כִּי לֹא חָמֵץ כִּי גֹרְשׁוּ מִמִּצְרַיִם וְלֹא יָכְלוּ לְהִתְמַהְמֵהַּ וְגַם צֵדָה לֹא עָשׂוּ לָהֶם:

יגביה את המרור להראותו למסובין כשאומר את זה

מָרוֹר זֶה שֶׁאָנוּ אוֹכְלִים עַל שׁוּם מָה. עַל שׁוּם שֶׁמֵּרְרוּ הַמִּצְרִים אֶת חַיֵּי אֲבוֹתֵינוּ בְּמִצְרַיִם. שֶׁנֶּאֱמַר וַיְמָרְרוּ אֶת חַיֵּיהֶם בַּעֲבֹדָה קָשָׁה בְּחֹמֶר וּבִלְבֵנִים וּבְכָל עֲבֹדָה בַּשָּׂדֶה אֵת כָּל עֲבֹדָתָם אֲשֶׁר עָבְדוּ בָהֶם בְּפָרֶךְ:

• • • •➤ ━━━━━ ━ • ━━━━━ ◀• • • •

On one occasion, Doctor Herman found himself treating two men for the same severe illness. Both patients, Yosef Katz and Binyamin Rokeach, were placed in the same room so that Doctor Herman could see to both their needs at once. Yosef and Binyamin got to know each other quite well as they both underwent surgery, then began the slow, painful process towards recovery. Doctor Herman treated each man with the utmost consideration, helping them feel more comfortable and easing their pain in any way he could.

After a week or so, Binyamin noticed somewhat uneasily that Doctor Herman seemed to give Yosef more individual attention. He set a wrapped glass of ice on Yosef's night stand each evening, and assured him that he could call if he awakened in the night. Binyamin could not help wondering why Doctor Herman thought that Yosef deserved the extra attention, even though both were in identical situations.

After several days, Binyamin finally worked up the courage to address the question while Doctor Herman treated him. "Excuse me," he said timidly. "Please don't take this the wrong way; believe me when I say that there are no words to express how much I appreciate everything you've done for me! But I can't help noticing that you've

Lift the middle matzah up, display it to the assmebled people and say

his matzah we eat — what is the reason? Because the dough of our ancestors did not have
time to become leavened before the King of
kings, the Holy Blessed One, revealed Himself to them
and redeemed them, as it is written, "They baked matzah
cakes from the dough that they had brought out of Egypt
because it had not risen; for they had been driven out of
Egypt and could not delay; nor had they prepared and
[other] provisions for themselves."

Lift the maror and say

his maror we eat — what is the reason? Because
the Egyptians embittered the lives of our ancestors in Egypt, as it is written, "They made [the
Jews'] lives bitter with hard service, with mortar and with
bricks, and with all manner of service in the field; their entire service at which they made them slave vigorously."

· · · ▸ ━━━━ ● · ━━━━ ◂ · · ·

been a little more attentive to Yosef, and I was wondering why. After
all, we're both in the same situation."

Doctor Herman gave the sick man a reassuring smile and placed a
friendly hand on his shoulder. "Binyamin, allow me to explain. Because
of my familiarity with your illness, I know what to generally expect:
when you will be in pain, when you will be cold or hot, when you need
extra attention. Based on that knowledge, I do everything I can for you.

"But what if there's something else you need? I can't read minds; I
can only work with what I know! And in this case, Yosef has specifically told me that he's troubled by nightmares and must take a cold
drink of water before he can fall asleep again. Since he can't rise from
his bed to get the water, I've started putting ice water by his bed each
evening in case he'll need it during the night. That's also why I've told

בְּכָל דּוֹר וָדוֹר חַיָּב אָדָם לִרְאוֹת אֶת עַצְמוֹ כְּאִלּוּ הוּא יָצָא מִמִּצְרַיִם שֶׁנֶּאֱמַר וְהִגַּדְתָּ לְבִנְךָ בַּיּוֹם הַהוּא לֵאמֹר בַּעֲבוּר זֶה עָשָׂה יי לִי בְּצֵאתִי מִמִּצְרָיִם. לֹא אֶת אֲבוֹתֵינוּ בִּלְבָד גָּאַל הַקָּדוֹשׁ בָּרוּךְ הוּא אֶלָּא אַף אוֹתָנוּ גָּאַל עִמָּהֶם. שֶׁנֶּאֱמַר וְאוֹתָנוּ הוֹצִיא מִשָּׁם. לְמַעַן הָבִיא אֹתָנוּ לָתֶת לָנוּ אֶת הָאָרֶץ אֲשֶׁר נִשְׁבַּע לַאֲבֹתֵינוּ:

him that he should feel free to call me in the night, if he needs to talk about his nightmares."

Doctor Herman looked at Binyamin with sympathy. "It's not a matter of favoring one of you over the other, you understand; it's simply that Yosef has verbally expressed what he needs, and I am therefore able to give him more personalized assistance."

❋ ❋ ❋

While we have expressed our gratitude in *Dayeinu* for the numerous miracles that Hashem performed for us, Rabban Gamliel emphasizes that there is nothing as powerful as verbal acknowledgment and appreciation. Because these three points represent the greatest aspects of the miracles of Pesach, Rabban Gamliel teaches that we must speak aloud regarding Pesach, *matzah* and *maror* in order to fulfill our obligation.

In every generation, a person is obligated to regard himself as though he himself had actually left Egypt...

After the previous emphasis on our obligation to thank Hashem for His kindness, why does the *Baal Haggadah* reiterate this point?

❋ ❋ ❋

R' Yisrael was easily the most popular man in the city. He was a philanthropist, whose wealth was matched only by his generous heart; he was a person of exemplary character, who had not allowed his money to change his friendly modest manner; he

n every generation, a person is obligated to regard himself as if he had gone out of Egypt, as
implied [in Exodus], "It is because of this, that
Hashem did for me when I went out of Egypt." It was not
only our ancestors whom the Holy Blessed One redeemed
from Egypt; rather He redeemed us together with them,
as implied [in Deuteronomy] "He brought us out from
there, so that He might bring us to the land He promised
our fathers and give it to us."

showed the greatest respect for Torah scholars, and was scrupulous
about setting aside time each day to study Torah himself; and he offered not only generous contributions to anyone who needed, but a
sympathetic ear and excellent advice.

Many people, as they spoke about him with the utmost respect and
admiration, suggested that his marvelous personality was a direct result of his humble beginnings. R' Yisrael's father had been a simple
pauper who made his way from *shul* to *shul*, seeking alms from the
people who came to pray. The good-natured blessings that his father
had received had eventually achieved fruition in his son, R' Yisrael. It
was only natural that a man who knew poverty in his childhood
would want to share his good fortune with the indigent.

One day, a close friend of R' Yisrael asked for permission to speak
to him frankly. "I have your best interests in mind," the friend explained, "but I don't want you to be insulted."

"By all means," R' Yisrael replied. "What is it?"

"As you know," the friend began, "money is one of the *yetzer hara's*
favorite tools of corruption. A person who is blessed with wealth can
sometimes be blinded by the glitter of coins and grow impatient with
those that are less fortunate."

"Go on," R' Yisrael urged.

"When I was here yesterday," the friend continued, choosing his
words carefully, "you were talking to R' Michel about how much

יכסה המצות ויגביה הכוס בידו ויאמר

לְפִיכָךְ אֲנַחְנוּ חַיָּבִים לְהוֹדוֹת לְהַלֵּל לְשַׁבֵּחַ לְפָאֵר לְרוֹמֵם לְהַדֵּר לְבָרֵךְ לְעַלֵּה וּלְקַלֵּס לְמִי שֶׁעָשָׂה לַאֲבוֹתֵינוּ וְלָנוּ אֶת כָּל הַנִּסִּים הָאֵלּוּ. הוֹצִיאָנוּ מֵעַבְדוּת לְחֵרוּת. מִיָּגוֹן לְשִׂמְחָה. וּמֵאֵבֶל לְיוֹם טוֹב. וּמֵאֲפֵלָה לְאוֹר גָּדוֹל. וּמִשִּׁעְבּוּד לִגְאֻלָּה. וְנֹאמַר לְפָנָיו שִׁירָה חֲדָשָׁה הַלְלוּיָהּ:

money he needs to marry off his daughter. Forgive me for saying this, but you were a bit less patient than you usually are under such circumstances. I just wanted to bring it to your attention, R' Yisrael. I hope you'll forgive me."

"Not only do I forgive you, my friend, but I thank you," R' Yisrael said with the utmost sincerity. "I truly appreciate your consideration in bringing the matter to my attention."

Three days later, the townspeople reeled at the sight of R' Yisrael, dressed in tattered clothing, trudging from door to door and asking for alms! He collected a substantial amount of money from the astonished people, money that he promptly distributed to the poor. Out of respect for R' Yisrael, no one asked him directly what he was doing; but the whispers ran from one side of the city to the next as everyone wondered why the richest man in town would do such a thing.

When a family member asked for an explanation, R' Yisrael readily replied, "I've always remembered what it was like when I was a child, when we never knew where the next crust of bread would come from. It's the memory of those feelings that help me sympathize with those that come to me now for help. In order to hold fast to those memories, to recall what it's like to worry about your next meal, I have decided to periodically don the clothing of a pauper and make my humble rounds around the city, begging for alms. In this way, I can be sure that I won't lose the proper perspective."

After enumerating the many acts of kindness that Hashem did for us, we are commanded to verbally mention the Pesach

Cover the matzos and raise the cup

herefore, we are obligated to thank, praise, to laud, to glorify, to exalt, to adore, to bless and to acclaim the One Who did all these miracles for our fathers and for us. He took us out from slavery to freedom, from sorrow to joy, from mourning to festivity, from deep darkness to great illumination and from servitude to redemption. Therefore let us recite a new son before Him: Praise Hashem.*

sacrifice, the *matzah* and the *maror,* to ensure that we are truly fulfilling our obligation of gratitude to Hashem. Then, by considering ourselves as if we were actually in Egypt and had participated in the redemption, we come to a deeper understanding of the gratitude we must feel towards Hashem for taking *Klal Yisrael* out of Egypt — a gratitude magnified by the previous declaration that if Hashem had not taken the Jews out of Egypt, we would still be enslaved today.

Therefore, we are obligated to thank, praise...

Why does the *Baal Haggadah* use the word "Therefore"? To what does this refer?

Hashem had blessed Gavriel with an incredible talent: his ability to play the violin. His haunting music evoked the deepest emotions from his listeners. He never played professionally at public affairs; as a young child, he had decided that it would be inappropriate to use Hashem's gift for anything other than inspiring others to Hashem's service. Instead, he played only for small groups — on Purim, at times when a friend was in need of encouragement, sometimes even for great Torah leaders who requested his presence at a *Melave Malkah.*

As Gavriel grew older, he earned a name as a respected Torah schol-ar. He eventually married and raised a beautiful family. The violin re-mained carefully stored in its case, brought out only on rare occasions.

At one point, Gavriel suddenly found himself beset on all sides. His modest business suffered a terrible loss, leaving him without a source of income; he and one of his children contracted a serious med-ical condition that demanded expensive medications and frequent medical consultations; and his oldest daughter reached marriageable age, forcing him to consider the costs of a wedding and a dowry. Still, Gavriel refused to despair, even as he tried to discover a way to meet his many bills and get himself back on his feet. The violin often sang in those days as Gavriel played of his faith and trust in Hashem.

Then, as suddenly as his problems had begun, they ended. Someone invested heavily in his business and his creditors stopped pressuring him to pay his debts immediately. The doctors told him that they were will-ing to wait for their fees and arranged for him to receive a discount for the medicines. Gavriel joyfully shared the good news with his wife and family, praising Hashem for turning the wheel of fortune in their favor.

That Shabbos, Gavriel accidentally overheard a conversation be-tween two of his neighbors. He listened with astonishment as he heard one of them remark that R' Hershel Grossman had spoken to his doctors and convinced them to give him more time to pay his medical bills. No wonder the doctors had been so generous!

Gavriel wondered how he could express his appreciation to R' Her-shel for his kind intervention on his behalf. Then, remembering R' Hershel's love for music, Gavriel smiled.

That night, after *havdalah*, Gavriel appeared at R' Hershel's home, carrying his treasured violin. As the family sat down to eat their *Melave Malkah*, Gavriel played joyous tunes of praise. R' Hershel and his family listened to the impromptu concert with great enjoyment, relishing the beautiful music.

As Gavriel took his leave of the Grossman family, he quietly thanked R' Hershel for interceding with the doctors on his behalf. "You helped me out when I truly needed it," he said gratefully.

R' Hershel smiled and waved his hand. "Please, Gavriel. The last thing I want is for you to feel indebted to me! All I did was talk to a few old friends of mine. I was glad to be of assistance."

Over the course of the following week, Gavriel discovered exactly how much R' Hershel had done for him. Not only did he speak with the doctors, but he had also persuaded several people to invest in Gavriel's business and convinced his creditors to stop pressuring him! Awed by R' Hershel's generosity and his modest dismissal of what he'd done, Gavriel remembered the music he played and felt ashamed. How small and paltry his gesture of appreciation appeared, now that he knew exactly how much R' Hershel had done for him!

"Well," Gavriel said with determination, "this week will be different."

He sat down and worked for hours, composing the most beautiful music. He added words to the haunting tunes, thanking Hashem for sending him a messenger as trustworthy as R' Hershel to help him in his time of need.

That *motzaei* Shabbos, Gavriel appeared once again in the Grossman home and played the violin as he never had in all his life. Tears streamed openly down R' Hershel's face at the haunting sounds of the incredible music that stole its way directly into his soul.

"Thank you," he told Gavriel, his voice trembling with emotion. "But tell me, why did you return tonight, and why was the music so much more powerful?"

Gavriel gently closed his violin case. "R' Hershel, last week when I played for you, it was a thank you for persuading my doctors to give me some leeway in making my payments. But since then, R' Hershel, I have discovered that you have done so much more for my family and me. Last week wasn't enough. Now that I know how much you've done on my behalf, I can try to express my full gratitude and appreciation!"

The *Baal Haggadah* has enumerated all the wonders that Hashem accomplished on our behalf — the miracles of *Dayeinu*; the specific aspects of Pesach, *matzah* and *maror*; our consideration that we, ourselves, were redeemed from Egypt. Now we can say "therefore" — because of all this, we can praise, exalt and glorify Hashem with the words of *Hallel*.

In fact, one can suggest that the methods by which we list

הַלְלוּיָה הַלְלוּ עַבְדֵי יי הַלְלוּ אֶת שֵׁם יי: יְהִי שֵׁם יי מְבֹרָךְ
מֵעַתָּה וְעַד עוֹלָם: מִמִּזְרַח שֶׁמֶשׁ עַד מְבוֹאוֹ מְהֻלָּל שֵׁם יי:
רָם עַל כָּל גּוֹיִם יי עַל הַשָּׁמַיִם כְּבוֹדוֹ: מִי כַּיי אֱלֹהֵינוּ הַמַּגְבִּיהִי לָשָׁבֶת:
הַמַּשְׁפִּילִי לִרְאוֹת בַּשָּׁמַיִם וּבָאָרֶץ: מְקִימִי מֵעָפָר דָּל מֵאַשְׁפֹּת יָרִים
אֶבְיוֹן: לְהוֹשִׁיבִי עִם נְדִיבִים עִם נְדִיבֵי עַמּוֹ: מוֹשִׁיבִי עֲקֶרֶת הַבַּיִת אֵם
הַבָּנִים שְׂמֵחָה הַלְלוּיָה:

Hashem's praises — the fourteen stanzas of *Dayeinu* — cor-
respond to the fourteen paragraphs of prayer and praise, as
listed below, with which we thank Hashem for what He has
done for us:

*Hallelukah (Tehillim 113); Betzeis (114); Shefoch (79); Lo lanu
(115); Hashem zecharanu (116); Ahavti (116); Ma Ashiv (116); Hal-
lelu (117); Hodu (118); Hodu Lashem (136); Nishmas; Shochen ad;
Uvemakhalos; Yishtabach.*

Indeed, it is because of our recognition of His greatness that
we come to sing His praises!

Hallelukah! Praise...
When Israel went out of Egypt...

The *Baal Haggadah* concludes the section of *Maggid* with two sec-
tions from *Hallel* and a blessing of redemption. Then the *Hallel* is interrupted by the festive meal; we continue to recite Hashem's praises
after the meal and the *Afikoman* have been concluded. Why did the
Baal Haggadah choose to begin with two praises, pause for the festive
meal, and then continue with more praises?

The young boy eagerly ripped open the bag of potato chips. He
paused just long enough to mumble a halfhearted *berachah* before he stuffed half the contents into his mouth.
He was still busy chewing when a hand landed gently on his

raise Hashem! Servants of Hashem — offer praise; praise the name of Hashem. May Hashem's Name be blessed from now until eternity. From the rising of the sun until its setting, Hashem's name be praised. Hashem is exalted above all nations; His glory is over the heavens. Who is like Hashem, our G-d, Who dwells on high, yet lowers Himself to look down on the heaven and earth. He raises the poor from the dust; He lists the needy form the trash heap to seat them with nobles, with the nobles of His people. He restores the barren woman to the house, into a joyful mother of children, praise Hashem!*

shoulder. Turning, he stared with shock at the sight of R' Shmuel Feivelberg standing next to him with a gentle smile. The boy almost choked as he tried to swallow his mouthful as quickly as possible.

"What's your name?" R' Shmuel asked warmly.

"B-Baruch," the boy gasped, trying not to gawk with awe at the most prominent man in the community. Close to ninety years old, R' Shmuel was known for his scholarship, his wisdom, and his genuine caring for every single Jew he ever met. And now he was talking to him!

"Could we sit down, Baruch, and talk for a few minutes?"

"Of course," Baruch said quickly. He followed the elderly man to a nearby bench, where they sat down together.

R' Shmuel paused for a moment, as if gathering his thoughts. "You know, Baruch," he began, "the Torah tells us that Yitzchak *Avinu* asked Eisav, 'Make delicacies for me such as I love, and bring it to me and I will eat, so that my soul may bless you before I die.'

"Now, Chazal tell us that if a person makes a proper blessing on his food; eats for the sake of Heaven; and learns Torah while he eats, his meal is actually considered like a sacrifice on the *mizbeyach*! So you see, Baruch, eating can actually elevate a person, just as Yitzchak *Avinu* wanted to reach a higher level to bless his son through eating a meal that Eisav prepared for him.

בְּצֵאת יִשְׂרָאֵל מִמִּצְרָיִם בֵּית יַעֲקֹב מֵעַם לֹעֵז: הָיְתָה יְהוּדָה לְקָדְשׁוֹ יִשְׂרָאֵל מַמְשְׁלוֹתָיו: הַיָּם רָאָה וַיָּנֹס הַיַּרְדֵּן יִסֹּב לְאָחוֹר: הֶהָרִים רָקְדוּ כְאֵילִים גְּבָעוֹת כִּבְנֵי צֹאן: מַה לְּךָ הַיָּם כִּי תָנוּס הַיַּרְדֵּן תִּסֹּב לְאָחוֹר: הֶהָרִים תִּרְקְדוּ כְאֵילִים גְּבָעוֹת כִּבְנֵי צֹאן: מִלִּפְנֵי אָדוֹן חוּלִי אָרֶץ מִלִּפְנֵי אֱלוֹהַּ יַעֲקֹב: הַהֹפְכִי הַצּוּר אֲגַם מָיִם חַלָּמִישׁ לְמַעְיְנוֹ מָיִם:

אוחז הכוס בידו עד גאל ישראל ואומר בשמחה עצומה

בָּרוּךְ אַתָּה יי אֱלֹהֵינוּ מֶלֶךְ הָעוֹלָם אֲשֶׁר גְּאָלָנוּ וְגָאַל אֶת אֲבוֹתֵינוּ מִמִּצְרַיִם וְהִגִּיעָנוּ הַלַּיְלָה הַזֶּה לֶאֱכָל בּוֹ מַצָּה וּמָרוֹר. כֵּן יי אֱלֹהֵינוּ וֵאלֹהֵי אֲבוֹתֵינוּ יַגִּיעֵנוּ לְמוֹעֲדִים וְלִרְגָלִים אֲחֵרִים הַבָּאִים לִקְרָאתֵנוּ לְשָׁלוֹם שְׂמֵחִים בְּבִנְיַן עִירֶךָ וְשָׂשִׂים בַּעֲבוֹדָתֶךָ. וְנֹאכַל שָׁם מִן הַזְּבָחִים וּמִן הַפְּסָחִים (במוצ"ש יש אומרים מִן הַפְּסָחִים וּמִן הַזְּבָחִים) אֲשֶׁר יַגִּיעַ דָּמָם עַל קִיר מִזְבַּחֲךָ לְרָצוֹן וְנוֹדֶה לְךָ שִׁיר חָדָשׁ עַל גְּאֻלָּתֵנוּ וְעַל פְּדוּת נַפְשֵׁנוּ: בָּרוּךְ אַתָּה יי גָּאַל יִשְׂרָאֵל:

"On the other hand," R' Shmuel continued, "Hashem does not look favorably upon a person who uses his food just for the sake of satisfying his own desires."

Baruch hung his head, realizing the truth of R' Shmuel's gentle rebuke. "I understand," he whispered, looking down at the half-eaten bag of chips. "I'll try to do better next time, really I will!"

"I'm glad to hear that," R' Shmuel smiled, patting the young boy on the arm. "And don't forget, your name is 'Baruch,' which means 'blessing.' Hashem is surely counting on you to make your *berachos*, and your eating habits, extra special!"

❀ ❀ ❀

Through our appreciation of Hashem's great kindness and miracles, we come to praise Him; but the *Baal Haggadah* interrupts that praise to introduce the festive meal, which, if

hen Israel went out of Egypt, the House of Jacob from a people of a foreign language, Judah became His holy one, Israel His dominion. *The sea saw and fled; the Jordan turned backward. The mountains skipped like rams, the hills like young lambs. What is with you, O Sea, that you flee? Jordan, [why] do you turn backward? Mountains, why do you skip like rams; hills [why] like young lambs? [We do so] before the Master, the Creator of the earth, before Hashem of Jacob; the One Who turns the rock into a pool of water, the flint-stone into a stream of water.*

Hold the cup of wine and say

lessed are You Hashem, our G-d, King of the Universe Who redeemed us and redeemed our ancestors from Egypt and has enabled us to reach this night so that we may eat matzah and maror on it. So too Hashem, our G-d and G-d of our fathers, enable us to reach other festivals and holidays that will come to us in peace, celebrating in the rebuilding of Your city and rejoicing in Your service. Then we shall eat of the sacrifices and of the Paschal offerings (when Peasch falls on Saturday night: of the Paschal offerings and the sacrifices), whose blood shall be sprinkled on the wall of Your altar to be graciously accepted. Then we shall sing a new song for our redemption and for the deliverance of our souls. Blessed are You Hashem, who redeemed Israel.*

eaten in the proper manner, will elevate us to even greater heights. Once we have completed the festive meal and eaten the *Afikoman*, we can resume our praises of Hashem on an even higher level than before.

בָּרוּךְ אַתָּה יי, אֱלֹהֵינוּ מֶלֶךְ הָעוֹלָם, בּוֹרֵא פְּרִי הַגָּפֶן:

ושותה בהסיבת שמאל ואינו מברך אחריו

רָחְצָה

בָּרוּךְ אַתָּה יי, אֱלֹהֵינוּ מֶלֶךְ הָעוֹלָם, אֲשֶׁר קִדְּשָׁנוּ
בְּמִצְוֹתָיו, וְצִוָּנוּ עַל נְטִילַת יָדָיִם:

מוֹצִיא

בָּרוּךְ אַתָּה יי, אֱלֹהֵינוּ מֶלֶךְ הָעוֹלָם, הַמּוֹצִיא לֶחֶם מִן
הָאָרֶץ:

מַצָּה

בָּרוּךְ אַתָּה יי, אֱלֹהֵינוּ מֶלֶךְ הָעוֹלָם, אֲשֶׁר קִדְּשָׁנוּ
בְּמִצְוֹתָיו, וְצִוָּנוּ עַל אֲכִילַת מַצָּה:

מָרוֹר

בָּרוּךְ אַתָּה יי, אֱלֹהֵינוּ מֶלֶךְ הָעוֹלָם, אֲשֶׁר קִדְּשָׁנוּ
בְּמִצְוֹתָיו, וְצִוָּנוּ עַל אֲכִילַת מָרוֹר:

כּוֹרֵךְ

זֵכֶר לְמִקְדָּשׁ כְּהִלֵּל. כֵּן עָשָׂה הִלֵּל, בִּזְמַן שֶׁבֵּית הַמִּקְדָּשׁ
הָיָה קַיָּם, הָיָה כּוֹרֵךְ (פֶּסַח) מַצָּה וּמָרוֹר וְאוֹכְלָם
בְּיַחַד. לְקַיֵּם מַה שֶׁנֶּאֱמַר עַל מַצּוֹת וּמְרוֹרִים יֹאכְלֻהוּ:

שֻׁלְחָן עוֹרֵךְ

צָפוּן

בָּרֵךְ

שִׁיר הַמַּעֲלוֹת. בְּשׁוּב יי אֶת שִׁיבַת צִיּוֹן הָיִינוּ כְּחֹלְמִים:
אָז יִמָּלֵא שְׂחוֹק פִּינוּ וּלְשׁוֹנֵנוּ רִנָּה. אָז יֹאמְרוּ בַגּוֹיִם הִגְדִּיל
יי לַעֲשׂוֹת עִם אֵלֶּה: הִגְדִּיל יי לַעֲשׂוֹת עִמָּנוּ. הָיִינוּ שְׂמֵחִים: שׁוּבָה יי
אֶת שְׁבִיתֵנוּ כַּאֲפִיקִים בַּנֶּגֶב: הַזֹּרְעִים בְּדִמְעָה בְּרִנָּה יִקְצֹרוּ: הָלוֹךְ
יֵלֵךְ וּבָכֹה נֹשֵׂא מֶשֶׁךְ הַזָּרַע. בֹּא יָבֹא בְרִנָּה. נֹשֵׂא אֲלֻמֹּתָיו:

הַמְזַמֵּן אוֹמֵר: רַבּוֹתַי נְבָרֵךְ:
הַמְסֻבִּים עוֹנִים: יְהִי שֵׁם יי מְבֹרָךְ מֵעַתָּה וְעַד עוֹלָם:
הַמְזַמֵּן חוֹזֵר: יְהִי שֵׁם יי מְבֹרָךְ מֵעַתָּה וְעַד עוֹלָם:
בִּרְשׁוּת מָרָנָן וְרַבָּנָן וְרַבּוֹתַי נְבָרֵךְ (בעשרה אֱלֹהֵינוּ) שֶׁאָכַלְנוּ מִשֶּׁלּוֹ:
וְאוֹמְרִים הַמְסֻבִּים וְאח״כ הַמְבָרֵךְ: בָּרוּךְ (בעשרה אֱלֹהֵינוּ) שֶׁאָכַלְנוּ מִשֶּׁלּוֹ
וּבְטוּבוֹ חָיִינוּ:

בָּרוּךְ אַתָּה יי אֱלֹהֵינוּ מֶלֶךְ הָעוֹלָם. הַזָּן אֶת הָעוֹלָם כֻּלּוֹ. בְּטוּבוֹ
בְּחֵן בְּחֶסֶד וּבְרַחֲמִים. הוּא נוֹתֵן לֶחֶם לְכָל בָּשָׂר. כִּי לְעוֹלָם
חַסְדּוֹ: וּבְטוּבוֹ הַגָּדוֹל תָּמִיד לֹא חָסַר לָנוּ וְאַל יֶחְסַר לָנוּ מָזוֹן לְעוֹלָם
וָעֶד. בַּעֲבוּר שְׁמוֹ הַגָּדוֹל. כִּי הוּא אֵל זָן וּמְפַרְנֵס לַכֹּל וּמֵטִיב לַכֹּל
וּמֵכִין מָזוֹן לְכָל בְּרִיּוֹתָיו אֲשֶׁר בָּרָא: (כָּאָמוּר פּוֹתֵחַ אֶת יָדֶךָ
וּמַשְׂבִּיעַ לְכָל חַי רָצוֹן:) בָּרוּךְ אַתָּה יי. הַזָּן אֶת הַכֹּל:

נוֹדֶה לְךָ יי אֱלֹהֵינוּ. עַל שֶׁהִנְחַלְתָּ לַאֲבוֹתֵינוּ אֶרֶץ חֶמְדָּה טוֹבָה
וּרְחָבָה. וְעַל שֶׁהוֹצֵאתָנוּ יי אֱלֹהֵינוּ מֵאֶרֶץ מִצְרַיִם. וּפְדִיתָנוּ
מִבֵּית עֲבָדִים. וְעַל בְּרִיתְךָ שֶׁחָתַמְתָּ בִּבְשָׂרֵנוּ. וְעַל תּוֹרָתְךָ שֶׁלִּמַּדְתָּנוּ.
וְעַל חֻקֶּיךָ שֶׁהוֹדַעְתָּנוּ. וְעַל חַיִּים חֵן וָחֶסֶד שֶׁחוֹנַנְתָּנוּ. וְעַל אֲכִילַת
מָזוֹן שָׁאַתָּה זָן וּמְפַרְנֵס אוֹתָנוּ תָּמִיד. בְּכָל יוֹם וּבְכָל עֵת וּבְכָל שָׁעָה:

וְעַל הַכֹּל יי אֱלֹהֵינוּ אֲנַחְנוּ מוֹדִים לָךְ וּמְבָרְכִים אוֹתָךְ. יִתְבָּרַךְ
שִׁמְךָ בְּפִי כָּל חַי תָּמִיד לְעוֹלָם וָעֶד: כַּכָּתוּב: וְאָכַלְתָּ וְשָׂבָעְתָּ
וּבֵרַכְתָּ אֶת יי אֱלֹהֶיךָ עַל הָאָרֶץ הַטֹּבָה אֲשֶׁר נָתַן לָךְ: בָּרוּךְ אַתָּה יי.
עַל הָאָרֶץ וְעַל הַמָּזוֹן:

רַחֵם (נָא) יי אֱלֹהֵינוּ עַל יִשְׂרָאֵל עַמֶּךָ. וְעַל יְרוּשָׁלַיִם עִירֶךָ. וְעַל
צִיּוֹן מִשְׁכַּן כְּבוֹדֶךָ. וְעַל מַלְכוּת בֵּית דָּוִד מְשִׁיחֶךָ. וְעַל הַבַּיִת

הַגָּדוֹל וְהַקָּדוֹשׁ שֶׁנִּקְרָא שְׁמְךָ עָלָיו: אֱלֹהֵינוּ. אָבִינוּ. רְעֵנוּ זוּנֵנוּ פַּרְנְסֵנוּ וְכַלְכְּלֵנוּ וְהַרְוִיחֵנוּ. וְהַרְוַח לָנוּ יי אֱלֹהֵינוּ מְהֵרָה מִכָּל צָרוֹתֵינוּ. וְנָא אַל תַּצְרִיכֵנוּ יי אֱלֹהֵינוּ לֹא לִידֵי מַתְּנַת בָּשָׂר וָדָם וְלֹא לִידֵי הַלְוָאָתָם. כִּי אִם לְיָדְךָ הַמְּלֵאָה. הַפְּתוּחָה. הַקְּדוֹשָׁה וְהָרְחָבָה. שֶׁלֹא נֵבוֹשׁ וְלֹא נִכָּלֵם לְעוֹלָם וָעֶד:

בשבת אומרים:

רְצֵה וְהַחֲלִיצֵנוּ יי אֱלֹהֵינוּ בְּמִצְוֹתֶיךָ וּבְמִצְוַת יוֹם הַשְּׁבִיעִי הַשַּׁבָּת הַגָּדוֹל וְהַקָּדוֹשׁ הַזֶּה כִּי יוֹם זֶה גָּדוֹל וְקָדוֹשׁ הוּא לְפָנֶיךָ לִשְׁבָּת בּוֹ וְלָנוּחַ בּוֹ בְּאַהֲבָה כְּמִצְוַת רְצוֹנֶךָ וּבִרְצוֹנְךָ הָנִיחַ לָנוּ יי אֱלֹהֵינוּ שֶׁלֹא תְהֵא צָרָה וְיָגוֹן וַאֲנָחָה בְּיוֹם מְנוּחָתֵנוּ וְהַרְאֵנוּ יי אֱלֹהֵינוּ בְּנֶחָמַת צִיּוֹן עִירֶךָ וּבְבִנְיַן יְרוּשָׁלַיִם עִיר קָדְשֶׁךָ כִּי אַתָּה הוּא בַּעַל הַיְשׁוּעוֹת וּבַעַל הַנֶּחָמוֹת:

אֱלֹהֵינוּ וֵאלֹהֵי אֲבוֹתֵינוּ יַעֲלֶה וְיָבוֹא וְיַגִּיעַ וְיֵרָאֶה וְיֵרָצֶה וְיִשָּׁמַע וְיִפָּקֵד וְיִזָּכֵר זִכְרוֹנֵנוּ וּפִקְדוֹנֵנוּ וְזִכְרוֹן אֲבוֹתֵינוּ וְזִכְרוֹן מָשִׁיחַ בֶּן דָּוִד עַבְדֶּךָ וְזִכְרוֹן יְרוּשָׁלַיִם עִיר קָדְשֶׁךָ וְזִכְרוֹן כָּל עַמְּךָ בֵּית יִשְׂרָאֵל לְפָנֶיךָ לִפְלֵיטָה לְטוֹבָה לְחֵן וּלְחֶסֶד וּלְרַחֲמִים לְחַיִּים וּלְשָׁלוֹם בְּיוֹם חַג הַמַּצּוֹת הַזֶּה. זָכְרֵנוּ יי אֱלֹהֵינוּ בּוֹ לְטוֹבָה וּפָקְדֵנוּ בּוֹ לִבְרָכָה וְהוֹשִׁיעֵנוּ בוֹ לְחַיִּים. וּבִדְבַר יְשׁוּעָה וְרַחֲמִים חוּס וְחָנֵּנוּ וְרַחֵם עָלֵינוּ וְהוֹשִׁיעֵנוּ כִּי אֵלֶיךָ עֵינֵינוּ כִּי אֵל מֶלֶךְ חַנּוּן וְרַחוּם אָתָּה:

וּבְנֵה יְרוּשָׁלַיִם עִיר הַקֹּדֶשׁ בִּמְהֵרָה בְיָמֵינוּ. בָּרוּךְ אַתָּה יי. בּוֹנֵה בְרַחֲמָיו יְרוּשָׁלָיִם: אָמֵן:

בָּרוּךְ אַתָּה יי אֱלֹהֵינוּ מֶלֶךְ הָעוֹלָם. הָאֵל. אָבִינוּ. מַלְכֵּנוּ. אַדִּירֵנוּ. בּוֹרְאֵנוּ. גּוֹאֲלֵנוּ. יוֹצְרֵנוּ. קְדוֹשֵׁנוּ קְדוֹשׁ יַעֲקֹב. רוֹעֵנוּ רוֹעֵה יִשְׂרָאֵל. הַמֶּלֶךְ הַטּוֹב וְהַמֵּטִיב לַכֹּל. שֶׁבְּכָל יוֹם וָיוֹם הוּא הֵטִיב הוּא מֵטִיב הוּא יֵיטִיב לָנוּ. הוּא גְמָלָנוּ הוּא גוֹמְלֵנוּ הוּא יִגְמְלֵנוּ לָעַד לְחֵן וּלְחֶסֶד וּלְרַחֲמִים וּלְרֶוַח. הַצָּלָה וְהַצְלָחָה. בְּרָכָה וִישׁוּעָה. נֶחָמָה. פַּרְנָסָה וְכַלְכָּלָה. וְרַחֲמִים וְחַיִּים וְשָׁלוֹם וְכָל טוֹב. וּמִכָּל טוּב לְעוֹלָם אַל יְחַסְּרֵנוּ.

הָרַחֲמָן הוּא יִמְלֹךְ עָלֵינוּ לְעוֹלָם וָעֶד: הָרַחֲמָן הוּא יִתְבָּרַךְ בַּשָּׁמַיִם וּבָאָרֶץ: הָרַחֲמָן הוּא יִשְׁתַּבַּח לְדוֹר דּוֹרִים.

וְיִתְפָּאַר בָּנוּ לָעַד וּלְנֵצַח נְצָחִים. וְיִתְהַדַּר בָּנוּ לָעַד וּלְעוֹלְמֵי עוֹלָמִים: הָרַחֲמָן הוּא יְפַרְנְסֵנוּ בְּכָבוֹד: הָרַחֲמָן הוּא יִשְׁבֹּר עֻלֵּנוּ מֵעַל צַוָּארֵנוּ וְהוּא יוֹלִיכֵנוּ קוֹמְמִיּוּת לְאַרְצֵנוּ: הָרַחֲמָן הוּא יִשְׁלַח לָנוּ בְּרָכָה מְרֻבָּה בַּבַּיִת הַזֶּה וְעַל שֻׁלְחָן זֶה שֶׁאָכַלְנוּ עָלָיו: הָרַחֲמָן הוּא יִשְׁלַח לָנוּ אֶת אֵלִיָּהוּ הַנָּבִיא זָכוּר לַטּוֹב וִיבַשֶּׂר לָנוּ בְּשׂוֹרוֹת טוֹבוֹת יְשׁוּעוֹת וְנֶחָמוֹת: הָרַחֲמָן הוּא יְבָרֵךְ אֶת (אָבִי מוֹרִי) בַּעַל הַבַּיִת הַזֶּה וְאֶת (אִמִּי מוֹרָתִי) בַּעֲלַת הַבַּיִת הַזֶּה. אוֹתָם וְאֶת בֵּיתָם וְאֶת זַרְעָם וְאֶת כָּל אֲשֶׁר לָהֶם. (וְאִם סָמוּךְ עַל שֻׁלְחָן עַצְמוֹ יֹאמַר: הָרַחֲמָן הוּא יְבָרֵךְ אוֹתִי וְאֶת אִשְׁתִּי וְאֶת זַרְעִי וְאֶת כָּל אֲשֶׁר לִי), אוֹתָנוּ וְאֶת כָּל אֲשֶׁר לָנוּ. כְּמוֹ שֶׁנִּתְבָּרְכוּ אֲבוֹתֵינוּ אַבְרָהָם יִצְחָק וְיַעֲקֹב, בַּכֹּל. מִכֹּל. כֹּל. כֵּן יְבָרֵךְ אוֹתָנוּ כֻּלָּנוּ יַחַד בִּבְרָכָה שְׁלֵמָה. וְנֹאמַר אָמֵן:

בַּמָּרוֹם יְלַמְּדוּ עֲלֵיהֶם וְעָלֵינוּ זְכוּת שֶׁתְּהֵא לְמִשְׁמֶרֶת שָׁלוֹם. וְנִשָּׂא בְרָכָה מֵאֵת יְיָ. וּצְדָקָה מֵאֱלֹהֵי יִשְׁעֵנוּ. וְנִמְצָא חֵן וְשֵׂכֶל טוֹב בְּעֵינֵי אֱלֹהִים וְאָדָם:

לשבת: הָרַחֲמָן הוּא יַנְחִילֵנוּ יוֹם שֶׁכֻּלּוֹ שַׁבָּת וּמְנוּחָה לְחַיֵּי הָעוֹלָמִים:

הָרַחֲמָן הוּא יַנְחִילֵנוּ יוֹם שֶׁכֻּלּוֹ טוֹב:

הָרַחֲמָן הוּא יְזַכֵּנוּ לִימוֹת הַמָּשִׁיחַ וּלְחַיֵּי הָעוֹלָם הַבָּא: מִגְדּוֹל יְשׁוּעוֹת מַלְכּוֹ וְעֹשֶׂה חֶסֶד לִמְשִׁיחוֹ לְדָוִד וּלְזַרְעוֹ עַד עוֹלָם: עֹשֶׂה שָׁלוֹם בִּמְרוֹמָיו הוּא יַעֲשֶׂה שָׁלוֹם עָלֵינוּ וְעַל כָּל יִשְׂרָאֵל וְאִמְרוּ אָמֵן:

יְראוּ אֶת יְיָ קְדֹשָׁיו כִּי אֵין מַחְסוֹר לִירֵאָיו: כְּפִירִים רָשׁוּ וְרָעֵבוּ וְדֹרְשֵׁי יְיָ לֹא יַחְסְרוּ כָל טוֹב: הוֹדוּ לַייָ כִּי טוֹב כִּי לְעוֹלָם חַסְדּוֹ: פּוֹתֵחַ אֶת יָדֶךָ וּמַשְׂבִּיעַ לְכָל חַי רָצוֹן: בָּרוּךְ הַגֶּבֶר אֲשֶׁר יִבְטַח בַּיְיָ וְהָיָה יְיָ מִבְטַחוֹ: נַעַר הָיִיתִי גַּם זָקַנְתִּי וְלֹא רָאִיתִי צַדִּיק נֶעֱזָב וְזַרְעוֹ מְבַקֶּשׁ לָחֶם: יְיָ עֹז לְעַמּוֹ יִתֵּן יְיָ יְבָרֵךְ אֶת עַמּוֹ בַשָּׁלוֹם:

בָּרוּךְ אַתָּה יְיָ, אֱלֹהֵינוּ מֶלֶךְ הָעוֹלָם, בּוֹרֵא פְּרִי הַגָּפֶן:

ושותה בהסיבת שמאל ואינו מברך אחריו

מוזגים כוס רביעי ונוהגים לפתוח את הדלת

שְׁפֹךְ חֲמָתְךָ אֶל הַגּוֹיִם אֲשֶׁר לֹא יְדָעוּךָ וְעַל מַמְלָכוֹת אֲשֶׁר
בְּשִׁמְךָ לֹא קָרָאוּ: כִּי אָכַל אֶת יַעֲקֹב וְאֶת נָוֵהוּ הֵשַׁמּוּ:
שְׁפָךְ עֲלֵיהֶם זַעְמֶךָ וַחֲרוֹן אַפְּךָ יַשִּׂיגֵם: תִּרְדֹּף בְּאַף וְתַשְׁמִידֵם
מִתַּחַת שְׁמֵי יי:

Pour out your wrath upon the nations...

Why is this second half of *Hallel* introduced with *Shefoch chamascha*,
and what is its significance?

K asdale was a rough town. No one lived there if they could
help it. Some were tied down to their jobs; others simply
couldn't afford anything better. But it was the small Jewish
population that found life in Kasdale hardest, for many of the people
blamed their difficulties on the Jews.

The children suffered the most. While their parents had to ignore
sneers and slurs, the Jewish boys often found themselves the targets
of physical attacks; sometimes with stones, sometimes with fists.
Some of them crept fearfully through the streets, their jackets pulled
over their heads in a futile effort to hide. Even those that walked more
openly didn't dare go out alone.

Once, the boys gathered together to discuss the situation. "There
must be something we can do to stop it," one boy sighed.

"Maybe we should try to be friends with them," another boy suggested dubiously. "A little flattery and some small bribes might make
a big difference. If they see us as boys like themselves, it might stop
all the beatings."

The others were doubtful about the plan, but they couldn't think of
anything better. They decided to give it a try.

That afternoon, they spotted one of the rougher neighborhood boys
loitering near the candy shop. Gathering their courage, they ap-
proached the young thug and began a conversation.

Pour the fourth cup. It is customary to open the door and say:

**our out Your wrath upon the nations that do not ac-
knowledge You and upon the kingdoms that do not
call upon Your Name, for they have devoured Jacob
and destroyed his dwelling. Pour out Your anger agianst them,
and let the wrath of Your fury overtake them. Pursue them
with anger and destroy them from beneath Hashem's heaven.**

* * * ▶ ━━ ━ • ━ ━ ◀ * * * ·

"Hey, is there some way we could join you guys? You know, be friends?" One of the boys pulled a large chocolate bar out of his pocket and tossed it at the surly youth. "We're not so bad, once you get to know us."

The boy stuffed the chocolate bar into his pocket and eyed the anxious group of Jewish boys with a speculative gaze. "I'll have to discuss it with the rest of the gang," he said gruffly. "Ask me again tomorrow."

The following day, the boy returned. As the Jewish boys gathered around him, anxious to hear if their plan was working, he held up a grimy hand. "If you want to be part of the gang, you're gonna have to prove yourselves," he declared. "Be at the corner of 10th Street tonight at eight o'clock. Bring lots of chocolate and stuff." His eyes gleamed. "Then we'll see."

Hoping for the best, the group of Jewish boys appeared at the corner of 10th street at the stroke of eight. Less than five minutes later, they spotted the gang, five of the toughest boys in town, striding towards them. The expressions on their faces didn't seem very promising.

As the gang came closer, the boys' hearts sank. There was no sign of conciliation in their expressions; on the contrary, the sticks gripped in their fists spoke of a different language.

"Came with chocolate and other goodies, did ya?" the head of the gang sneered. "Well, hand it over, and quick! Or we'll give you something to help speed things up." He slapped the stick against his palm for emphasis.

The boys didn't waste any time trying to argue. They emptied their

הַלֵּל

לֹא לָנוּ יי לֹא לָנוּ כִּי לְשִׁמְךָ תֵּן כָּבוֹד עַל חַסְדְּךָ עַל אֲמִתֶּךָ: לָמָּה יֹאמְרוּ הַגּוֹיִם אַיֵּה נָא אֱלֹהֵיהֶם: וֵאלֹהֵינוּ בַשָּׁמָיִם כֹּל אֲשֶׁר חָפֵץ עָשָׂה: עֲצַבֵּיהֶם כֶּסֶף וְזָהָב מַעֲשֵׂה יְדֵי אָדָם: פֶּה לָהֶם וְלֹא יְדַבֵּרוּ עֵינַיִם לָהֶם וְלֹא יִרְאוּ: אָזְנַיִם לָהֶם וְלֹא יִשְׁמָעוּ אַף לָהֶם וְלֹא יְרִיחוּן: יְדֵיהֶם וְלֹא יְמִישׁוּן רַגְלֵיהֶם וְלֹא יְהַלֵּכוּ לֹא יֶהְגּוּ בִּגְרוֹנָם: כְּמוֹהֶם יִהְיוּ עֹשֵׂיהֶם כֹּל אֲשֶׁר בֹּטֵחַ בָּהֶם: יִשְׂרָאֵל בְּטַח בַּיי עֶזְרָם וּמָגִנָּם הוּא: בֵּית אַהֲרֹן בִּטְחוּ בַיי עֶזְרָם וּמָגִנָּם הוּא: יִרְאֵי יי בִּטְחוּ בַיי עֶזְרָם וּמָגִנָּם הוּא:

יי זְכָרָנוּ יְבָרֵךְ יְבָרֵךְ אֶת בֵּית יִשְׂרָאֵל יְבָרֵךְ אֶת בֵּית אַהֲרֹן: יְבָרֵךְ יִרְאֵי יי הַקְּטַנִּים עִם הַגְּדֹלִים: יֹסֵף יי עֲלֵיכֶם עֲלֵיכֶם

• • • • ◦ ▸ ━ ━ ━ • ◦ ━ ━ ◂ ◦ • • • •

pockets and fled, grateful to escape without any bruises.

The unhappy situation continued until a new Jewish family moved to Kasdale. The new family had three teenaged boys, all of them tall and unusually strong. The other Jewish boys welcomed their new friends with delight, hoping they could do something to improve their current state of misery.

When the three brothers heard about the gang that terrorized the Jewish children of the neighborhood, they laughed. "Don't worry!" they assured their new friends. "Our father always tells us that Hashem gave us our strength to be used for good reasons. This certainly qualifies!"

That very day, the three brothers, together with their new friends, set out in search of the gang of five. They found the group in an alleyway and managed to surprise them completely. The five thugs, usually so aggressive and rough when they faced younger, smaller adversaries, found themselves backing away in fear from these tall, hulking Jewish boys.

"We're here now," the eldest told the gang in a soft, menacing tone. "G-d sent us here to make sure you stop beating up Jewish kids in this neighborhood. The next time someone gets hurt, you're going to have to answer to us!"

וְעַל בְּנֵיכֶם: בְּרוּכִים אַתֶּם לַיי עשֵׂה שָׁמַיִם וָאָרֶץ: הַשָּׁמַיִם שָׁמַיִם
לַיי וְהָאָרֶץ נָתַן לִבְנֵי אָדָם: לֹא הַמֵּתִים יְהַלְלוּ יָהּ וְלֹא כָּל יֹרְדֵי
דוּמָה: וַאֲנַחְנוּ נְבָרֵךְ יָהּ מֵעַתָּה וְעַד עוֹלָם הַלְלוּיָהּ:

אָהַבְתִּי כִּי יִשְׁמַע יי אֶת קוֹלִי תַּחֲנוּנָי: כִּי הִטָּה אָזְנוֹ לִי וּבְיָמַי
אֶקְרָא: אֲפָפוּנִי חֶבְלֵי מָוֶת וּמְצָרֵי שְׁאוֹל מְצָאוּנִי צָרָה
וְיָגוֹן אֶמְצָא: וּבְשֵׁם יי אֶקְרָא אָנָּא יי מַלְּטָה נַפְשִׁי: חַנּוּן יי וְצַדִּיק
וֵאלֹהֵינוּ מְרַחֵם: שֹׁמֵר פְּתָאִים יי דַּלּוֹתִי וְלִי יְהוֹשִׁיעַ: שׁוּבִי נַפְשִׁי
לִמְנוּחָיְכִי כִּי יי גָּמַל עָלָיְכִי: כִּי חִלַּצְתָּ נַפְשִׁי מִמָּוֶת אֶת עֵינִי מִן
דִּמְעָה אֶת רַגְלִי מִדֶּחִי: אֶתְהַלֵּךְ לִפְנֵי יי בְּאַרְצוֹת הַחַיִּים: הֶאֱמַנְתִּי
כִּי אֲדַבֵּר אֲנִי עָנִיתִי מְאֹד: אֲנִי אָמַרְתִּי בְחָפְזִי כָּל הָאָדָם כֹּזֵב:

The gang leader nodded his head in quick, jerky movements, too
frightened to say anything.

From that day on, things changed in Kasdale. The neighborhood
boys, who understood nothing but brute strength, developed a new
respect for the Jews. To the Jewish boys, this new turn of events was
nothing less than an overt miracle performed by Hashem. Inspired by
this marvelous change in their lives, the boys made a festive meal in
which they thanked and praised Hashem for saving them from their
miserable situation.

❖ ❖ ❖

As we envision the coming of *Mashiach* and the final redemption,
our praise for Hashem is preceded by our firm belief that He will ultimately punish the nations for their misdeeds and show the entire earth
that He is the true Master of the world. Therefore, *Hallel* is introduced
with *Shefoch chamascha*, our adamant trust that Hashem will redeem
us; with His ultimate power revealed, we can offer the ultimate praise.

מָה אָשִׁיב לַיי. כָּל תַּגְמוּלוֹהִי עָלָי: כּוֹס יְשׁוּעוֹת אֶשָּׂא.
וּבְשֵׁם יי אֶקְרָא: נְדָרַי לַיי אֲשַׁלֵּם. נֶגְדָה נָא לְכָל עַמּוֹ:
יָקָר בְּעֵינֵי יי. הַמָּוְתָה לַחֲסִידָיו: אָנָּה יי כִּי אֲנִי עַבְדֶּךָ. אֲנִי
עַבְדְּךָ בֶּן אֲמָתֶךָ פִּתַּחְתָּ לְמוֹסֵרָי: לְךָ אֶזְבַּח זֶבַח תּוֹדָה.
וּבְשֵׁם יי אֶקְרָא: נְדָרַי לַיי אֲשַׁלֵּם. נֶגְדָה נָא לְכָל עַמּוֹ:
בְּחַצְרוֹת בֵּית יי. בְּתוֹכֵכִי יְרוּשָׁלָיִם. הַלְלוּיָהּ:

הַלְלוּ אֶת יי כָּל גּוֹיִם. שַׁבְּחוּהוּ כָּל הָאֻמִּים: כִּי גָבַר עָלֵינוּ
חַסְדּוֹ. וֶאֱמֶת יי לְעוֹלָם. הַלְלוּיָהּ:

כִּי לְעוֹלָם חַסְדּוֹ:	הוֹדוּ לַיי כִּי טוֹב
כִּי לְעוֹלָם חַסְדּוֹ:	יֹאמַר נָא יִשְׂרָאֵל
כִּי לְעוֹלָם חַסְדּוֹ:	יֹאמְרוּ נָא בֵית אַהֲרֹן
כִּי לְעוֹלָם חַסְדּוֹ:	יֹאמְרוּ נָא יִרְאֵי יי

מִן הַמֵּצַר קָרָאתִי יָּהּ. עָנָנִי בַמֶּרְחַב יָהּ: יי לִי לֹא אִירָא.
מַה יַּעֲשֶׂה לִי אָדָם: יי לִי בְּעֹזְרָי. וַאֲנִי אֶרְאֶה בְשֹׂנְאָי:
טוֹב לַחֲסוֹת בַּיי. מִבְּטֹחַ בָּאָדָם: טוֹב לַחֲסוֹת בַּיי. מִבְּטֹחַ
בִּנְדִיבִים: כָּל גּוֹיִם סְבָבוּנִי. בְּשֵׁם יי כִּי אֲמִילַם: סַבּוּנִי גַם
סְבָבוּנִי. בְּשֵׁם יי כִּי אֲמִילַם: סַבּוּנִי כִדְבוֹרִים. דֹּעֲכוּ כְּאֵשׁ
קוֹצִים. בְּשֵׁם יי כִּי אֲמִילַם: דָּחֹה דְחִיתַנִי לִנְפֹּל. וַיי עֲזָרָנִי:
עָזִּי וְזִמְרָת יָהּ. וַיְהִי לִי לִישׁוּעָה: קוֹל רִנָּה וִישׁוּעָה בְּאָהֳלֵי
צַדִּיקִים. יְמִין יי עֹשָׂה חָיִל: יְמִין יי רוֹמֵמָה. יְמִין יי עֹשָׂה
חָיִל: לֹא אָמוּת כִּי אֶחְיֶה. וַאֲסַפֵּר מַעֲשֵׂי יָהּ: יַסֹּר יִסְּרַנִי יָּהּ.

וַלַמֶּוֶת לֹא נְתָנָנִי : פִּתְחוּ לִי שַׁעֲרֵי צֶדֶק. אָבֹא בָם אוֹדֶה יָהּ : זֶה הַשַּׁעַר לַיְיָ. צַדִּיקִים יָבֹאוּ בוֹ :

אוֹדְךָ כִּי עֲנִיתָנִי. וַתְּהִי לִי לִישׁוּעָה. אוֹדְךָ כִּי עֲנִיתָנִי. וַתְּהִי לִי לִישׁוּעָה : אֶבֶן מָאֲסוּ הַבּוֹנִים. הָיְתָה לְרֹאשׁ פִּנָּה. אֶבֶן מָאֲסוּ הַבּוֹנִים. הָיְתָה לְרֹאשׁ פִּנָּה : מֵאֵת יְיָ הָיְתָה זֹּאת. הִיא נִפְלָאת בְּעֵינֵינוּ. מֵאֵת יְיָ הָיְתָה זֹּאת. הִיא נִפְלָאת בְּעֵינֵינוּ : זֶה הַיּוֹם עָשָׂה יְיָ. נָגִילָה וְנִשְׂמְחָה בוֹ. זֶה הַיּוֹם עָשָׂה יְיָ. נָגִילָה וְנִשְׂמְחָה בוֹ :

אָנָּא יְיָ הוֹשִׁיעָה נָּא :

אָנָּא יְיָ הוֹשִׁיעָה נָּא :

אָנָּא יְיָ הַצְלִיחָה נָּא :

אָנָּא יְיָ הַצְלִיחָה נָּא :

בָּרוּךְ הַבָּא בְּשֵׁם יְיָ. בֵּרַכְנוּכֶם מִבֵּית יְיָ. בָּרוּךְ הַבָּא בְּשֵׁם יְיָ. בֵּרַכְנוּכֶם מִבֵּית יְיָ. אֵל יְיָ וַיָּאֶר לָנוּ. אִסְרוּ חַג בַּעֲבֹתִים. עַד קַרְנוֹת הַמִּזְבֵּחַ. אֵל יְיָ וַיָּאֶר לָנוּ. אִסְרוּ חַג בַּעֲבֹתִים. עַד קַרְנוֹת הַמִּזְבֵּחַ. אֵלִי אַתָּה וְאוֹדֶךָּ. אֱלֹהַי אֲרוֹמְמֶךָּ. אֵלִי אַתָּה וְאוֹדֶךָּ. אֱלֹהַי אֲרוֹמְמֶךָּ. הוֹדוּ לַיְיָ כִּי טוֹב. כִּי לְעוֹלָם חַסְדּוֹ. הוֹדוּ לַיְיָ כִּי טוֹב. כִּי לְעוֹלָם חַסְדּוֹ :

הוֹדוּ לַיְיָ כִּי טוֹב.	כִּי לְעוֹלָם חַסְדּוֹ :
הוֹדוּ לֵאלֹהֵי הָאֱלֹהִים.	כִּי לְעוֹלָם חַסְדּוֹ :
הוֹדוּ לַאֲדֹנֵי הָאֲדֹנִים.	כִּי לְעוֹלָם חַסְדּוֹ :
לְעֹשֵׂה נִפְלָאוֹת גְּדֹלוֹת לְבַדּוֹ.	כִּי לְעוֹלָם חַסְדּוֹ :

כִּי לְעוֹלָם חַסְדּוֹ :   לְעֹשֵׂה הַשָּׁמַיִם בִּתְבוּנָה

כִּי לְעוֹלָם חַסְדּוֹ :   לְרֹקַע הָאָרֶץ עַל הַמָּיִם

כִּי לְעוֹלָם חַסְדּוֹ :   לְעֹשֵׂה אוֹרִים גְּדֹלִים

כִּי לְעוֹלָם חַסְדּוֹ :   אֶת הַשֶּׁמֶשׁ לְמֶמְשֶׁלֶת בַּיּוֹם

כִּי לְעוֹלָם חַסְדּוֹ :   אֶת הַיָּרֵחַ וְכוֹכָבִים לְמֶמְשְׁלוֹת בַּלָּיְלָה

כִּי לְעוֹלָם חַסְדּוֹ :   לְמַכֵּה מִצְרַיִם בִּבְכוֹרֵיהֶם

כִּי לְעוֹלָם חַסְדּוֹ :   וַיּוֹצֵא יִשְׂרָאֵל מִתּוֹכָם

כִּי לְעוֹלָם חַסְדּוֹ :   בְּיָד חֲזָקָה וּבִזְרוֹעַ נְטוּיָה

כִּי לְעוֹלָם חַסְדּוֹ :   לְגֹזֵר יַם סוּף לִגְזָרִים

כִּי לְעוֹלָם חַסְדּוֹ :   וְהֶעֱבִיר יִשְׂרָאֵל בְּתוֹכוֹ

כִּי לְעוֹלָם חַסְדּוֹ :   וְנִעֵר פַּרְעֹה וְחֵילוֹ בְיַם סוּף

כִּי לְעוֹלָם חַסְדּוֹ :   לְמוֹלִיךְ עַמּוֹ בַּמִּדְבָּר

כִּי לְעוֹלָם חַסְדּוֹ :   לְמַכֵּה מְלָכִים גְּדֹלִים

כִּי לְעוֹלָם חַסְדּוֹ :   וַיַּהֲרֹג מְלָכִים אַדִּירִים

כִּי לְעוֹלָם חַסְדּוֹ :   לְסִיחוֹן מֶלֶךְ הָאֱמֹרִי

כִּי לְעוֹלָם חַסְדּוֹ :   וּלְעוֹג מֶלֶךְ הַבָּשָׁן

כִּי לְעוֹלָם חַסְדּוֹ :   וְנָתַן אַרְצָם לְנַחֲלָה

כִּי לְעוֹלָם חַסְדּוֹ :   נַחֲלָה לְיִשְׂרָאֵל עַבְדּוֹ

כִּי לְעוֹלָם חַסְדּוֹ :   שֶׁבְּשִׁפְלֵנוּ זָכַר לָנוּ

כִּי לְעוֹלָם חַסְדּוֹ :   וַיִּפְרְקֵנוּ מִצָּרֵינוּ

כִּי לְעוֹלָם חַסְדּוֹ :   נֹתֵן לֶחֶם לְכָל בָּשָׂר

כִּי לְעוֹלָם חַסְדּוֹ :   הוֹדוּ לְאֵל הַשָּׁמָיִם

נִשְׁמַת כָּל חַי תְּבָרֵךְ אֶת שִׁמְךָ יְיָ אֱלֹהֵינוּ. וְרוּחַ כָּל בָּשָׂר תְּפָאֵר וּתְרוֹמֵם זִכְרְךָ מַלְכֵּנוּ תָּמִיד: מִן הָעוֹלָם וְעַד הָעוֹלָם אַתָּה אֵל. וּמִבַּלְעָדֶיךָ אֵין לָנוּ מֶלֶךְ גּוֹאֵל וּמוֹשִׁיעַ. פּוֹדֶה וּמַצִּיל וּמְפַרְנֵס וּמְרַחֵם בְּכָל עֵת צָרָה וְצוּקָה. אֵין לָנוּ מֶלֶךְ עוֹזֵר וְסוֹמֵךְ אֶלָּא אַתָּה: אֱלֹהֵי הָרִאשׁוֹנִים וְהָאַחֲרוֹנִים. אֱלוֹהַּ כָּל בְּרִיּוֹת. אֲדוֹן כָּל תּוֹלָדוֹת. הַמְהֻלָּל בְּרֹב הַתִּשְׁבָּחוֹת. הַמְנַהֵג עוֹלָמוֹ בְּחֶסֶד וּבְרִיּוֹתָיו בְּרַחֲמִים: וַייָ לֹא יָנוּם וְלֹא יִישָׁן. הַמְעוֹרֵר יְשֵׁנִים. וְהַמֵּקִיץ נִרְדָּמִים. וְהַמֵּשִׂיחַ אִלְּמִים. וְהַמַּתִּיר אֲסוּרִים. וְהַסּוֹמֵךְ נוֹפְלִים. וְהַזּוֹקֵף כְּפוּפִים. לְךָ לְבַדְּךָ אֲנַחְנוּ מוֹדִים: אִלּוּ פִינוּ מָלֵא שִׁירָה כַּיָּם. וּלְשׁוֹנֵנוּ רִנָּה כַּהֲמוֹן גַּלָּיו. וְשִׂפְתוֹתֵינוּ שֶׁבַח כְּמֶרְחֲבֵי רָקִיעַ. וְעֵינֵינוּ מְאִירוֹת כַּשֶּׁמֶשׁ וְכַיָּרֵחַ. וְיָדֵינוּ פְרוּשׂוֹת כְּנִשְׁרֵי שָׁמָיִם. וְרַגְלֵינוּ קַלּוֹת כָּאַיָּלוֹת. אֵין אֲנַחְנוּ מַסְפִּיקִים לְהוֹדוֹת לְךָ יְיָ אֱלֹהֵינוּ וֵאלֹהֵי אֲבוֹתֵינוּ. וּלְבָרֵךְ אֶת שְׁמֶךָ עַל אַחַת מֵאֶלֶף אַלְפֵי אֲלָפִים וְרִבֵּי רְבָבוֹת פְּעָמִים. הַטּוֹבוֹת שֶׁעָשִׂיתָ עִם אֲבוֹתֵינוּ וְעִמָּנוּ: מִמִּצְרַיִם גְּאַלְתָּנוּ יְיָ אֱלֹהֵינוּ. וּמִבֵּית עֲבָדִים פְּדִיתָנוּ. בְּרָעָב זַנְתָּנוּ. וּבְשָׂבָע כִּלְכַּלְתָּנוּ. מֵחֶרֶב הִצַּלְתָּנוּ. וּמִדֶּבֶר מִלַּטְתָּנוּ. וּמֵחֳלָיִם רָעִים וְנֶאֱמָנִים דִּלִּיתָנוּ: עַד הֵנָּה עֲזָרוּנוּ רַחֲמֶיךָ. וְלֹא עֲזָבוּנוּ חֲסָדֶיךָ וְאַל תִּטְּשֵׁנוּ יְיָ אֱלֹהֵינוּ לָנֶצַח: עַל כֵּן אֵבָרִים שֶׁפִּלַּגְתָּ בָּנוּ. וְרוּחַ וּנְשָׁמָה שֶׁנָּפַחְתָּ בְּאַפֵּינוּ. וְלָשׁוֹן אֲשֶׁר שַׂמְתָּ בְּפִינוּ. הֵן הֵם. יוֹדוּ וִיבָרְכוּ וִישַׁבְּחוּ וִיפָאֲרוּ וִירוֹמְמוּ וְיַעֲרִיצוּ וְיַקְדִּישׁוּ וְיַמְלִיכוּ אֶת שִׁמְךָ מַלְכֵּנוּ: כִּי כָל פֶּה לְךָ יוֹדֶה. וְכָל לָשׁוֹן לְךָ תִשָּׁבַע. וְכָל בֶּרֶךְ לְךָ תִכְרַע. וְכָל קוֹמָה לְפָנֶיךָ

תִּשְׁתַּחֲוֶה. וְכָל לְבָבוֹת יִירָאוּדְ. וְכָל קֶרֶב וּכְלָיוֹת יְזַמְּרוּ
לִשְׁמֶדְ. כַּדָּבָר שֶׁכָּתוּב. כָּל עַצְמוֹתַי תֹּאמַרְנָה יי מִי כָמוֹדְ.
מַצִּיל עָנִי מֵחָזָק מִמֶּנּוּ. וְעָנִי וְאֶבְיוֹן מִגֹּזְלוֹ. מִי יִדְמֶה לָדְ.
וּמִי יִשְׁוֶה לָּדְ. וּמִי יַעֲרָדְ לָדְ. הָאֵל הַגָּדוֹל הַגִּבּוֹר וְהַנּוֹרָא אֵל
עֶלְיוֹן. קוֹנֵה שָׁמַיִם וָאָרֶץ: נְהַלֶּלְדְ וּנְשַׁבֵּחֲדְ וּנְפָאֶרְדְ וּנְבָרֵדְ
אֶת שֵׁם קָדְשֶׁדְ. כָּאָמוּר, לְדָוִד, בָּרְכִי נַפְשִׁי אֶת יי. וְכָל קְרָבַי
אֶת שֵׁם קָדְשׁוֹ: הָאֵל בְּתַעֲצֻמוֹת עֻזֶּדְ. הַגָּדוֹל בִּכְבוֹד שְׁמֶדְ.
הַגִּבּוֹר לָנֶצַח וְהַנּוֹרָא בְּנוֹרְאוֹתֶיךָ: הַמֶּלֶךְ הַיּוֹשֵׁב עַל כִּסֵּא רָם
וְנִשָּׂא:

שׁוֹכֵן עַד מָרוֹם וְקָדוֹשׁ שְׁמוֹ. וְכָתוּב רַנְּנוּ צַדִּיקִים בַּיי.
לַיְשָׁרִים נָאוָה תְהִלָּה: בְּפִי יְשָׁרִים תִּתְהַלָּל. וּבְדִבְרֵי
צַדִּיקִים תִּתְבָּרַדְ. וּבִלְשׁוֹן חֲסִידִים תִּתְרוֹמָם. וּבְקֶרֶב
קְדוֹשִׁים תִּתְקַדָּשׁ:

וּבְמַקְהֲלוֹת רִבְבוֹת עַמְּדְ בֵּית יִשְׂרָאֵל. בְּרִנָּה יִתְפָּאַר
שִׁמְדְ מַלְכֵּנוּ בְּכָל דּוֹר וָדוֹר. שֶׁכֵּן חוֹבַת כָּל
הַיְצוּרִים. לְפָנֶיךָ יי אֱלֹהֵינוּ וֵאלֹהֵי אֲבוֹתֵינוּ. לְהוֹדוֹת לְהַלֵּל
לְשַׁבֵּחַ לְפָאֵר לְרוֹמֵם לְהַדֵּר לְבָרֵךְ לְעַלֵּה וּלְקַלֵּס. עַל כָּל דִּבְרֵי
שִׁירוֹת וְתִשְׁבָּחוֹת דָּוִד בֶּן יִשַׁי עַבְדְּדְ מְשִׁיחֶדְ:

יִשְׁתַּבַּח שִׁמְדְ לָעַד מַלְכֵּנוּ. הָאֵל הַמֶּלֶךְ הַגָּדוֹל וְהַקָּדוֹשׁ
בַּשָּׁמַיִם וּבָאָרֶץ. כִּי לְדְ נָאֶה יי אֱלֹהֵינוּ וֵאלֹהֵי
אֲבוֹתֵינוּ שִׁיר וּשְׁבָחָה. הַלֵּל וְזִמְרָה. עוֹז וּמֶמְשָׁלָה. נֶצַח גְּדֻלָּה

וּגְבוּרָה. תְּהִלָּה וְתִפְאֶרֶת. קְדֻשָּׁה וּמַלְכוּת : בְּרָכוֹת וְהוֹדָאוֹת מֵעַתָּה וְעַד עוֹלָם :

יְהַלְלוּךָ יי אֱלֹהֵינוּ עַל מַעֲשֶׂיךָ. וַחֲסִידֶיךָ צַדִּיקִים עוֹשֵׂי רְצוֹנֶךָ. וְכָל עַמְּךָ בֵּית יִשְׂרָאֵל. בְּרִנָּה יוֹדוּ וִיבָרְכוּ וִישַׁבְּחוּ וִיפָאֲרוּ וִירוֹמְמוּ וְיַעֲרִיצוּ וְיַקְדִּישׁוּ וְיַמְלִיכוּ אֶת שִׁמְךָ מַלְכֵּנוּ. כִּי לְךָ טוֹב לְהוֹדוֹת. וּלְשִׁמְךָ נָאֶה לְזַמֵּר. כִּי מֵעוֹלָם וְעַד עוֹלָם אַתָּה אֵל : בָּרוּךְ אַתָּה יי מֶלֶךְ מְהֻלָּל בַּתִּשְׁבָּחוֹת :

בָּרוּךְ אַתָּה יי, אֱלֹהֵינוּ מֶלֶךְ הָעוֹלָם, בּוֹרֵא פְּרִי הַגָּפֶן :

ושותה בהסיבת שמאל

בָּרוּךְ אַתָּה יי אֱלֹהֵינוּ מֶלֶךְ הָעוֹלָם עַל הַגֶּפֶן וְעַל פְּרִי הַגֶּפֶן וְעַל תְּנוּבַת הַשָּׂדֶה וְעַל אֶרֶץ חֶמְדָּה טוֹבָה וּרְחָבָה שֶׁרָצִיתָ וְהִנְחַלְתָּ לַאֲבוֹתֵינוּ לֶאֱכֹל מִפִּרְיָהּ וְלִשְׂבּוֹעַ מִטּוּבָהּ, רַחֵם (נָא) יי אֱלֹהֵינוּ עַל יִשְׂרָאֵל עַמֶּךָ וְעַל יְרוּשָׁלַיִם עִירֶךָ וְעַל צִיּוֹן מִשְׁכַּן כְּבוֹדֶךָ וְעַל מִזְבְּחֶךָ וְעַל הֵיכָלֶךָ, וּבְנֵה יְרוּשָׁלַיִם עִיר הַקֹּדֶשׁ בִּמְהֵרָה בְיָמֵינוּ וְהַעֲלֵנוּ לְתוֹכָהּ וְשַׂמְּחֵנוּ בְּבִנְיָנָהּ וְנֹאכַל מִפִּרְיָהּ וְנִשְׂבַּע מִטּוּבָהּ וּנְבָרֶכְךָ עָלֶיהָ בִּקְדֻשָּׁה וּבְטָהֳרָה : **בשבת:** וּרְצֵה וְהַחֲלִיצֵנוּ בְּיוֹם הַשַּׁבָּת הַזֶּה : וְשַׂמְּחֵנוּ בְּיוֹם חַג הַמַּצּוֹת הַזֶּה : כִּי אַתָּה יי טוֹב וּמֵטִיב לַכֹּל וְנוֹדֶה לְּךָ עַל הָאָרֶץ וְעַל פְּרִי הַגֶּפֶן : בָּרוּךְ אַתָּה יי עַל הָאָרֶץ וְעַל פְּרִי הַגֶּפֶן :

נִרְצָה

חֲסַל סִדּוּר פֶּסַח כְּהִלְכָתוֹ. כְּכָל מִשְׁפָּטוֹ וְחֻקָתוֹ. כַּאֲשֶׁר זָכִינוּ
לְסַדֵּר אוֹתוֹ. כֵּן נִזְכֶּה לַעֲשׂוֹתוֹ: זָךְ שׁוֹכֵן מְעוֹנָה. קוֹמֵם
קְהַל עֲדַת מִי מָנָה. בְּקָרוֹב נַהֵל נִטְעֵי כַנָּה. פְּדוּיִם לְצִיּוֹן בְּרִנָּה:

לְשָׁנָה הַבָּאָה בִּירוּשָׁלָיִם:

The Pesach seder has been completed...

What message does the *Baal Haggadah* offer us with this conclusion to the Pesach seder?

❊ ❊ ❊

Meshulam grinned to himself as he stuffed his costume into a bag. The big day had finally arrived. After weeks of rehearsals and hard work, he and his two closest friends were about to perform a play for the people of the neighborhood. How appropriate to stage an entertaining performance on *Shushan Purim* and then give all the proceeds to *tzedakah*!

Amram and Chaim greeted him excitedly as he hurried into the hall where the performance would take place. "Come on, get into your costume!" Amram urged. "You're the star of the show!"

Some fifteen minutes later, the curtains rose and the story began.

Meshulam played the part of Nachi, a boy living in Eastern Europe during the 17th century. When Nachi's *rebbe* reported that the boy was doing poorly in *cheder*, Nachi's father decided that it would be best to send his son to work.

"I'll apprentice him to Berel, the local shoemaker," Nachi's father declared. "He'll lead an honest, G-d fearing life. It's too much to hope that he'll ever become a Torah scholar!"

When Nachi discovered his father's plans for him, the boy was devastated. He tried to convince his father that he would improve his studies and really try harder, but his father was adamant. He refused to allow Nachi to waste his time, as well as the *rebbe's*, when he wasn't serious about his learning!

he Pesach Seder has been completed as the law commands; in accordance with all its rules and statutes; we were found worthy to observe it, so may we be worthy to observe it again. Pure One, Who dwells on high, raise up the congregation without number! Soon may You guide the stock You have planted, bringing them redeemed to Zion in Joyous song.

Next year in Jerusalem!

Nachi, realizing that his father would not believe that he really wanted to learn, decided to take matters into his own hands. He quietly packed a few belongings into a sack and crept out of his home one night, determined to make his way to a famous *yeshivah* in a nearby city.

Nachi had many adventures and hardships on his journey to the *yeshivah*, but he persevered. By the end of the play, Nachi had, indeed, grown to be a great Torah scholar, the pride of his parents and his city.

The play proved to be a great success. The boys were delighted to see that they had earned over one hundred dollars for *tzedakah*! The threesome beamed as they received dozens of compliments for the *tzedakah* they had collected as well as the important message their play had imparted.

That night, Meshulam's mother asked him how he felt about playing the part of Nachi.

"It was interesting, Mommy," the boy answered thoughtfully. "At first, I thought I was just playing a part. But when we practiced it over and over, I began to feel the way Nachi did. I spent so much time acting the part of Nachi, with his dedication to Torah study, that it became a part of me."

His mother smiled at him encouragingly as he added, "I think I'll be taking my own Torah learning a little more seriously from now on!"

❖ ❖ ❖

בליל ראשון אומרים פיוט זה

וּבְכֵן וַיְהִי בַּחֲצִי הַלַּיְלָה

בַּלַּיְלָה.	אָז רוֹב נִסִּים הִפְלֵאתָ
הַלַּיְלָה.	בְּרֹאשׁ אַשְׁמוּרוֹת זֶה
לַיְלָה.	גֵּר צֶדֶק נִצַּחְתּוֹ כְּנֶחֱלַק לוֹ

וַיְהִי בַּחֲצִי הַלַּיְלָה:

הַלַּיְלָה.	דַּנְתָּ מֶלֶךְ גְּרָר בַּחֲלוֹם
לַיְלָה.	הִפְחַדְתָּ אֲרַמִּי בְּאֶמֶשׁ
לַיְלָה.	וַיָּשַׂר יִשְׂרָאֵל לְמַלְאָךְ וַיּוּכַל לוֹ

וַיְהִי בַּחֲצִי הַלַּיְלָה:

הַלַּיְלָה.	זֶרַע בְּכוֹרֵי פַתְרוֹס מָחַצְתָּ בַּחֲצִי
בַּלַּיְלָה.	חֵילָם לֹא מָצְאוּ בְּקוּמָם
לַיְלָה.	טִיסַת נְגִיד חֲרוֹשֶׁת סִלִּיתָ בְּכוֹכְבֵי

וַיְהִי בַּחֲצִי הַלַּיְלָה:

בַּלַּיְלָה.	יָעַץ מְחָרֵף לְנוֹפֵף אִוּוּי הוֹבַשְׁתָּ פְגָרָיו
לַיְלָה.	כָּרַע בֵּל וּמַצָּבוֹ בְּאִישׁוֹן
לַיְלָה.	לְאִישׁ חֲמוּדוֹת נִגְלָה רָז חֲזוֹת

וַיְהִי בַּחֲצִי הַלַּיְלָה:

- - - ▸ ◆ — ◆ — ◀ ◂ - - -

As we conclude the Pesach *seder*, we rejoice that we have
merited to fulfill the *mitzvah* of Pesach night as we are commanded to do. However, we have done more than merely perform the *mitzvah*; we have elevated ourselves through fulfill-

מִשְׁתַּכֵּר בִּכְלֵי קֹדֶשׁ נֶהֱרַג בּוֹ **בַּלַּיְלָה.**

נוֹשַׁע מִבּוֹר אֲרָיוֹת פּוֹתֵר בְּעִתּוּתֵי **לַיְלָה.**

שִׂנְאָה נָטַר אֲגָגִי וְכָתַב סְפָרִים **בַּלַּיְלָה.**

וַיְהִי בַּחֲצִי הַלַּיְלָה:

עוֹרַרְתָּ נִצְחֲךָ עָלָיו בְּנֶדֶד שְׁנַת **לַיְלָה.**

פּוּרָה תִדְרוֹךְ לְשׁוֹמֵר מַה **מִּלַּיְלָה.**

צָרַח כַּשּׁוֹמֵר וְשָׂח אָתָא בֹקֶר וְגַם **לַיְלָה.**

וַיְהִי בַּחֲצִי הַלַּיְלָה:

קָרֵב יוֹם אֲשֶׁר הוּא לֹא יוֹם וְלֹא **לַיְלָה.**

רָם הוֹדַע כִּי לְךָ הַיּוֹם אַף לְךָ **הַלַּיְלָה.**

שׁוֹמְרִים הַפְקֵד לְעִירְךָ כָּל הַיּוֹם וְכָל **הַלַּיְלָה.**

תָּאִיר כְּאוֹר יוֹם חֶשְׁכַת **לַיְלָה.**

וַיְהִי בַּחֲצִי הַלַּיְלָה:

ing the commandment to relate the story of our redemption from Egypt. We ask Hashem that we merit to perform this *mitzvah* again in the future. We all beseech Him to allow us to achieve even higher levels of spirituality, until we may merit the true and final redemption — when we will be able to bring the Pesach sacrifice, just as our forefathers did, in the coming days of *Mashiach*!

Next Year in Yerushalayim!

בליל שני אומרים פיוט זה :

וּבְכֵן וַאֲמַרְתֶּם זֶבַח פֶּסַח:

בַּפֶּסַח. אֹמֶץ גְּבוּרוֹתֶיךָ הִפְלֵאתָ

פֶּסַח. בְּרֹאשׁ כָּל מוֹעֲדוֹת נִשֵּׂאתָ

פֶּסַח. גִּלִּיתָ לְאֶזְרָחִי חֲצוֹת לֵיל

וּבְכֵן וַאֲמַרְתֶּם זֶבַח פֶּסַח:

בַּפֶּסַח. דְּלָתָיו דָּפַקְתָּ כְּחוֹם הַיּוֹם

בַּפֶּסַח. הִסְעִיד נוֹצְצִים עֻגוֹת מַצּוֹת

פֶּסַח. וְאֶל הַבָּקָר רָץ זֵכֶר לְשׁוֹר עֵרֶךְ

וּבְכֵן וַאֲמַרְתֶּם זֶבַח פֶּסַח:

בַּפֶּסַח. זוֹעֲמוּ סְדוֹמִים וְלוֹהֲטוּ בָּאֵשׁ

פֶּסַח. חֻלַּץ לוֹט מֵהֶם וּמַצּוֹת אָפָה בְּקֵץ

בַּפֶּסַח. טָאטֵאתָ אַדְמַת מוֹף וְנוֹף בְּעָבְרְךָ

וּבְכֵן וַאֲמַרְתֶּם זֶבַח פֶּסַח:

פֶּסַח. יָהּ רֹאשׁ כָּל אוֹן מָחַצְתָּ בְּלֵיל שִׁמּוּר

פֶּסַח. כַּבִּיר עַל בֵּן בְּכוֹר פָּסַחְתָּ בְּדַם

בַּפֶּסַח. לְבִלְתִּי תֵּת מַחְית לָבֹא בִּפְסָחַי

וּבְכֵן וַאֲמַרְתֶּם זֶבַח פֶּסַח:

פֶּסַח. מְסֻגֶּרֶת סֻגְּרָה בְּעִתּוֹתֵי

פֶּסַח. נִשְׁמְדָה מִדְיָן בִּצְלִיל שְׂעוֹרֵי עֹמֶר

פֶּסַח. שֹׂרְפוּ מִשְׁמַנֵּי פּוּל וְלוּד בִּיקַד יְקוֹד

וּבְכֵן וַאֲמַרְתֶּם זֶבַח פֶּסַח:

פֶּסַח. עוֹד הַיּוֹם בְּנוֹב לַעֲמוֹד עַד גָּעָה עוֹנַת

בַּפֶּסַח. פַּס יָד כָּתְבָה לְקַעֲקֵעַ צוּל

בַּפֶּסַח. צָפֹה הַצָּפִית עָרוֹךְ הַשֻּׁלְחָן

וּבְכֵן וַאֲמַרְתֶּם זֶבַח פֶּסַח:

קָהָל כְּנִסָּה הֲדַסָּה צוֹם לְשַׁלֵּשׁ   **בַּפֶּסַח.**

רֹאשׁ מִבֵּית רָשָׁע מָחַצְתָּ בְּעֵץ חֲמִשִּׁים   **בַּפֶּסַח.**

שְׁתֵּי אֵלֶּה רֶגַע תָּבִיא לְעוּצִית   **בַּפֶּסַח.**

תָּעֹז יָדְךָ וְתָרוּם יְמִינֶךָ כְּלֵיל הִתְקַדֵּשׁ חַג   **פֶּסַח.**

וּבְכֵן וַאֲמַרְתֶּם זֶבַח פֶּסַח:

כִּי לוֹ נָאֶה, כִּי לוֹ יָאֶה.

אַדִּיר בִּמְלוּכָה, **בָּחוּר** כַּהֲלָכָה, **גְּדוּדָיו** יֹאמְרוּ לוֹ : לְךָ וּלְךָ, לְךָ כִּי לְךָ, לְךָ אַף לְךָ, לְךָ יְיָ הַמַּמְלָכָה. כִּי לוֹ נָאֶה, כִּי לוֹ יָאֶה.

דָּגוּל בִּמְלוּכָה, **הָדוּר** כַּהֲלָכָה, **וָתִיקָיו** יֹאמְרוּ לוֹ : לְךָ וּלְךָ, לְךָ כִּי לְךָ, לְךָ אַף לְךָ, לְךָ יְיָ הַמַּמְלָכָה. כִּי לוֹ נָאֶה, כִּי לוֹ יָאֶה.

זַכַּאי בִּמְלוּכָה, **חָסִין** כַּהֲלָכָה, **טַפְסְרָיו** יֹאמְרוּ לוֹ : לְךָ וּלְךָ, לְךָ כִּי לְךָ, לְךָ אַף לְךָ, לְךָ יְיָ הַמַּמְלָכָה. כִּי לוֹ נָאֶה, כִּי לוֹ יָאֶה.

יָחִיד בִּמְלוּכָה, **כַּבִּיר** כַּהֲלָכָה, **לִמּוּדָיו** יֹאמְרוּ לוֹ : לְךָ וּלְךָ, לְךָ כִּי לְךָ, לְךָ אַף לְךָ, לְךָ יְיָ הַמַּמְלָכָה. כִּי לוֹ נָאֶה, כִּי לוֹ יָאֶה.

מוֹשֵׁל בִּמְלוּכָה, **נוֹרָא** כַּהֲלָכָה, **סְבִיבָיו** יֹאמְרוּ לוֹ : לְךָ וּלְךָ, לְךָ כִּי לְךָ, לְךָ אַף לְךָ, לְךָ יְיָ הַמַּמְלָכָה. כִּי לוֹ נָאֶה, כִּי לוֹ יָאֶה.

עָנָו בִּמְלוּכָה, **פּוֹדֶה** כַּהֲלָכָה, **צַדִּיקָיו** יֹאמְרוּ לוֹ : לְךָ וּלְךָ, לְךָ כִּי לְךָ, לְךָ אַף לְךָ, לְךָ יְיָ הַמַּמְלָכָה. כִּי לוֹ נָאֶה, כִּי לוֹ יָאֶה.

קָדוֹשׁ בִּמְלוּכָה, **רַחוּם** כַּהֲלָכָה, **שִׁנְאַנָּיו** יֹאמְרוּ לוֹ : לְךָ וּלְךָ, לְךָ כִּי לְךָ, לְךָ אַף לְךָ, לְךָ יְיָ הַמַּמְלָכָה. כִּי לוֹ נָאֶה, כִּי לוֹ יָאֶה.

תַּקִּיף בִּמְלוּכָה, **תּוֹמֵךְ** כַּהֲלָכָה, **תְּמִימָיו** יֹאמְרוּ לוֹ : לְךָ וּלְךָ, לְךָ כִּי לְךָ, לְךָ אַף לְךָ, לְךָ יְיָ הַמַּמְלָכָה. כִּי לוֹ נָאֶה, כִּי לוֹ יָאֶה.

אַדִּיר הוּא יִבְנֶה בֵּיתוֹ בְּקָרוֹב. בִּמְהֵרָה בִּמְהֵרָה בְּיָמֵינוּ בְּקָרוֹב. אֵל בְּנֵה. אֵל בְּנֵה. בְּנֵה בֵּיתְךָ בְּקָרוֹב:

בָּחוּר הוּא. גָּדוֹל הוּא. דָּגוּל הוּא. יִבְנֶה בֵּיתוֹ בְּקָרוֹב. בִּמְהֵרָה בִּמְהֵרָה בְּיָמֵינוּ בְּקָרוֹב. אֵל בְּנֵה. אֵל בְּנֵה. בְּנֵה בֵּיתְךָ בְּקָרוֹב:

הָדוּר הוּא. וָתִיק הוּא. זַכַּאי הוּא. חָסִיד הוּא. יִבְנֶה בֵּיתוֹ בְּקָרוֹב. בִּמְהֵרָה בִּמְהֵרָה בְּיָמֵינוּ בְּקָרוֹב. אֵל בְּנֵה. אֵל בְּנֵה. בְּנֵה בֵּיתְךָ בְּקָרוֹב:

טָהוֹר הוּא. יָחִיד הוּא. כַּבִּיר הוּא. לָמוּד הוּא. מֶלֶךְ הוּא. נוֹרָא הוּא. סַגִּיב הוּא. עִזּוּז הוּא. פּוֹדֶה הוּא. צַדִּיק הוּא. יִבְנֶה בֵּיתוֹ בְּקָרוֹב. בִּמְהֵרָה בִּמְהֵרָה בְּיָמֵינוּ בְּקָרוֹב. אֵל בְּנֵה. אֵל בְּנֵה. בְּנֵה בֵּיתְךָ בְּקָרוֹב:

קָדוֹשׁ הוּא. רַחוּם הוּא. שַׁדַּי הוּא. תַּקִּיף הוּא. יִבְנֶה בֵּיתוֹ בְּקָרוֹב. בִּמְהֵרָה בִּמְהֵרָה בְּיָמֵינוּ בְּקָרוֹב. אֵל בְּנֵה. אֵל בְּנֵה. בְּנֵה בֵּיתְךָ בְּקָרוֹב:

אֶחָד מִי יוֹדֵעַ אֶחָד אֲנִי יוֹדֵעַ. אֶחָד אֱלֹהֵינוּ שֶׁבַּשָּׁמַיִם וּבָאָרֶץ:

שְׁנַיִם מִי יוֹדֵעַ שְׁנַיִם אֲנִי יוֹדֵעַ. שְׁנֵי לוּחוֹת הַבְּרִית. אֶחָד אֱלֹהֵינוּ שֶׁבַּשָּׁמַיִם וּבָאָרֶץ:

שְׁלֹשָׁה מִי יוֹדֵעַ. שְׁלֹשָׁה אֲנִי יוֹדֵעַ. שְׁלֹשָׁה אָבוֹת. שְׁנֵי לוּחוֹת הַבְּרִית. אֶחָד אֱלֹהֵינוּ שֶׁבַּשָּׁמַיִם וּבָאָרֶץ:

אַרְבַּע מִי יוֹדֵעַ. אַרְבַּע אֲנִי יוֹדֵעַ. אַרְבַּע אִמָּהוֹת. שְׁלֹשָׁה אָבוֹת. שְׁנֵי לוּחוֹת הַבְּרִית. אֶחָד אֱלֹהֵינוּ שֶׁבַּשָּׁמַיִם וּבָאָרֶץ:

חֲמִשָּׁה מִי יוֹדֵעַ. חֲמִשָּׁה אֲנִי יוֹדֵעַ. חֲמִשָּׁה חוּמְשֵׁי תוֹרָה. אַרְבַּע אִמָּהוֹת. שְׁלֹשָׁה אָבוֹת. שְׁנֵי לוּחוֹת הַבְּרִית. אֶחָד אֱלֹהֵינוּ שֶׁבַּשָּׁמַיִם וּבָאָרֶץ:

שִׁשָּׁה מִי יוֹדֵעַ. שִׁשָּׁה אֲנִי יוֹדֵעַ. שִׁשָּׁה סִדְרֵי מִשְׁנָה. חֲמִשָּׁה חוּמְשֵׁי תוֹרָה. אַרְבַּע אִמָּהוֹת. שְׁלֹשָׁה אָבוֹת. שְׁנֵי לוּחוֹת הַבְּרִית. אֶחָד אֱלֹהֵינוּ שֶׁבַּשָּׁמַיִם וּבָאָרֶץ:

שִׁבְעָה מִי יוֹדֵעַ. שִׁבְעָה אֲנִי יוֹדֵעַ. שִׁבְעָה יְמֵי שַׁבַּתָּא. שִׁשָּׁה סִדְרֵי מִשְׁנָה. חֲמִשָּׁה חוּמְשֵׁי תוֹרָה. אַרְבַּע אִמָּהוֹת. שְׁלֹשָׁה אָבוֹת. שְׁנֵי לוּחוֹת הַבְּרִית. אֶחָד אֱלֹהֵינוּ שֶׁבַּשָּׁמַיִם וּבָאָרֶץ:

שְׁמוֹנָה מִי יוֹדֵעַ. שְׁמוֹנָה אֲנִי יוֹדֵעַ. שְׁמוֹנָה יְמֵי מִילָה. שִׁבְעָה יְמֵי שַׁבַּתָּא. שִׁשָּׁה סִדְרֵי מִשְׁנָה. חֲמִשָּׁה חוּמְשֵׁי תוֹרָה. אַרְבַּע אִמָּהוֹת. שְׁלֹשָׁה אָבוֹת. שְׁנֵי לוּחוֹת הַבְּרִית. אֶחָד אֱלֹהֵינוּ שֶׁבַּשָּׁמַיִם וּבָאָרֶץ׃

תִּשְׁעָה מִי יוֹדֵעַ. תִּשְׁעָה אֲנִי יוֹדֵעַ. תִּשְׁעָה יַרְחֵי לֵדָה. שְׁמוֹנָה יְמֵי מִילָה. שִׁבְעָה יְמֵי שַׁבַּתָּא. שִׁשָּׁה סִדְרֵי מִשְׁנָה. חֲמִשָּׁה חוּמְשֵׁי תוֹרָה. אַרְבַּע אִמָּהוֹת. שְׁלֹשָׁה אָבוֹת. שְׁנֵי לוּחוֹת הַבְּרִית. אֶחָד אֱלֹהֵינוּ שֶׁבַּשָּׁמַיִם וּבָאָרֶץ׃

עֲשָׂרָה מִי יוֹדֵעַ. עֲשָׂרָה אֲנִי יוֹדֵעַ. עֲשָׂרָה דִבְּרַיָא. תִּשְׁעָה יַרְחֵי לֵדָה. שְׁמוֹנָה יְמֵי מִילָה. שִׁבְעָה יְמֵי שַׁבַּתָּא. שִׁשָּׁה סִדְרֵי מִשְׁנָה. חֲמִשָּׁה חוּמְשֵׁי תוֹרָה. אַרְבַּע אִמָּהוֹת. שְׁלֹשָׁה אָבוֹת. שְׁנֵי לוּחוֹת הַבְּרִית. אֶחָד אֱלֹהֵינוּ שֶׁבַּשָּׁמַיִם וּבָאָרֶץ׃

אַחַד עָשָׂר מִי יוֹדֵעַ. אַחַד עָשָׂר אֲנִי יוֹדֵעַ. אַחַד עָשָׂר כּוֹכְבַיָּא. עֲשָׂרָה דִבְּרַיָא. תִּשְׁעָה יַרְחֵי לֵדָה. שְׁמוֹנָה יְמֵי מִילָה. שִׁבְעָה יְמֵי שַׁבַּתָּא. שִׁשָּׁה סִדְרֵי מִשְׁנָה. חֲמִשָּׁה חוּמְשֵׁי תוֹרָה. אַרְבַּע אִמָּהוֹת. שְׁלֹשָׁה אָבוֹת. שְׁנֵי לוּחוֹת הַבְּרִית. אֶחָד אֱלֹהֵינוּ שֶׁבַּשָּׁמַיִם וּבָאָרֶץ׃

שְׁנֵים עָשָׂר מִי יוֹדֵעַ. שְׁנֵים עָשָׂר אֲנִי יוֹדֵעַ. שְׁנֵים עָשָׂר שִׁבְטַיָּא. אַחַד עָשָׂר כּוֹכְבַיָּא. עֲשָׂרָה דִבְּרַיָא. תִּשְׁעָה יַרְחֵי לֵדָה. שְׁמוֹנָה יְמֵי מִילָה. שִׁבְעָה יְמֵי שַׁבַּתָּא. שִׁשָּׁה סִדְרֵי מִשְׁנָה. חֲמִשָּׁה חוּמְשֵׁי תוֹרָה. אַרְבַּע אִמָּהוֹת. שְׁלֹשָׁה אָבוֹת. שְׁנֵי לוּחוֹת הַבְּרִית. אֶחָד אֱלֹהֵינוּ שֶׁבַּשָּׁמַיִם וּבָאָרֶץ׃

שְׁלֹשָׁה עָשָׂר מִי יוֹדֵעַ. שְׁלֹשָׁה עָשָׂר אֲנִי יוֹדֵעַ. שְׁלֹשָׁה עָשָׂר מִדַּיָּא. שְׁנֵים עָשָׂר שִׁבְטַיָּא. אַחַד עָשָׂר כּוֹכְבַיָּא. עֲשָׂרָה דִבְּרַיָא. תִּשְׁעָה יַרְחֵי לֵדָה. שְׁמוֹנָה יְמֵי מִילָה. שִׁבְעָה יְמֵי שַׁבַּתָּא. שִׁשָּׁה סִדְרֵי מִשְׁנָה. חֲמִשָּׁה חוּמְשֵׁי תוֹרָה. אַרְבַּע אִמָּהוֹת. שְׁלֹשָׁה אָבוֹת. שְׁנֵי לוּחוֹת הַבְּרִית. אֶחָד אֱלֹהֵינוּ שֶׁבַּשָּׁמַיִם וּבָאָרֶץ׃

חַד גַּדְיָא. חַד גַּדְיָא. דְּזַבִּין אַבָּא בִּתְרֵי זוּזֵי. חַד גַּדְיָא. חַד
גַּדְיָא:

וְאָתָא שׁוּנְרָא וְאָכְלָה לְגַדְיָא. דְּזַבִּין אַבָּא בִּתְרֵי זוּזֵי. חַד גַּדְיָא. חַד
גַּדְיָא:

וְאָתָא כַּלְבָּא וְנָשַׁךְ לְשׁוּנְרָא. דְּאָכַל לְגַדְיָא. דְּזַבִּין אַבָּא בִּתְרֵי זוּזֵי.
חַד גַּדְיָא. חַד גַּדְיָא:

וְאָתָא חוּטְרָא וְהִכָּה לְכַלְבָּא. דְּנָשַׁךְ לְשׁוּנְרָא. דְּאָכַל לְגַדְיָא. דְּזַבִּין
אַבָּא בִּתְרֵי זוּזֵי. חַד גַּדְיָא. חַד גַּדְיָא:

וְאָתָא נוּרָא וְשָׂרַף לְחוּטְרָא. דְּהִכָּה לְכַלְבָּא. דְּנָשַׁךְ לְשׁוּנְרָא. דְּאָכַל
לְגַדְיָא. דְּזַבִּין אַבָּא בִּתְרֵי זוּזֵי. חַד גַּדְיָא. חַד גַּדְיָא:

וְאָתָא מַיָּא וְכָבָה לְנוּרָא. דְּשָׂרַף לְחוּטְרָא. דְּהִכָּה לְכַלְבָּא. דְּנָשַׁךְ
לְשׁוּנְרָא. דְּאָכַל לְגַדְיָא. דְּזַבִּין אַבָּא בִּתְרֵי זוּזֵי. חַד גַּדְיָא. חַד גַּדְיָא:

***One little kid! one little kid! that my father bought for
two zuzim...***

Why was this passage added to the *Haggadah*? What message does
it carry?

❖ ❖ ❖

Reb Alter was a very old man. He had witnessed the coming
and passing of three generations over the course of his long,
fruitful life. Reb Alter himself wasn't sure of his exact age, but
he knew he was over one hundred and ten years old. People gathered
to listen to his priceless stories, for Reb Alter still possessed a sharp
mind and a wealth of historical knowledge.

On one such occasion, Reb Gershon came to visit the spry old man
and sat talking with him for hours. Over the course of the conversa-

וְאָתָא תוֹרָא וְשָׁתָה לְמַיָּא. דְּכָבָה לְנוּרָא. דְּשָׂרַף לְחוּטְרָא. דְּהִכָּה לְכַלְבָּא. דְּנָשַׁךְ לְשׁוּנְרָא. דְּאָכַל לְגַדְיָא. דְּזַבִּין אַבָּא בִּתְרֵי זוּזֵי. חַד גַּדְיָא. חַד גַּדְיָא:

וְאָתָא הַשּׁוֹחֵט וְשָׁחַט לְתוֹרָא. דְּשָׁתָה לְמַיָּא. דְּכָבָה לְנוּרָא. דְּשָׂרַף לְחוּטְרָא. דְּהִכָּה לְכַלְבָּא. דְּנָשַׁךְ לְשׁוּנְרָא. דְּאָכַל לְגַדְיָא. דְּזַבִּין אַבָּא בִּתְרֵי זוּזֵי. חַד גַּדְיָא. חַד גַּדְיָא:

וְאָתָא מַלְאַךְ הַמָּוֶת וְשָׁחַט לְשׁוֹחֵט. דְּשָׁחַט לְתוֹרָא. דְּשָׁתָה לְמַיָּא. דְּכָבָה לְנוּרָא. דְּשָׂרַף לְחוּטְרָא. דְּהִכָּה לְכַלְבָּא. דְּנָשַׁךְ לְשׁוּנְרָא. דְּאָכַל לְגַדְיָא. דְּזַבִּין אַבָּא בִּתְרֵי זוּזֵי. חַד גַּדְיָא. חַד גַּדְיָא:

וְאָתָא הַקָּדוֹשׁ בָּרוּךְ הוּא וְשָׁחַט לְמַלְאַךְ הַמָּוֶת דְּשָׁחַט לְשׁוֹחֵט. דְּשָׁחַט לְתוֹרָא. דְּשָׁתָה לְמַיָּא. דְּכָבָה לְנוּרָא. דְּשָׂרַף לְחוּטְרָא. דְּהִכָּה לְכַלְבָּא. דְּנָשַׁךְ לְשׁוּנְרָא. דְּאָכַל לְגַדְיָא. דְּזַבִּין אַבָּא בִּתְרֵי זוּזֵי. חַד גַּדְיָא. חַד גַּדְיָא:

tion, they touched upon the exquisite silver esrog box that was displayed in the main *shul*. "It's such a beautiful piece," Reb Gershon mused. "Where did it come from?"

"That's quite a long story," Reb Alter replied slowly, "and I don't think I've ever told it to anyone. Perhaps it's time to tell the story now."

Reb Gershon listened, fascinated, as Reb Alter began his tale.

❀ ❀ ❀

When I was a young boy, I often took quiet walks through the fields. On one such occasion, I witnessed a horrific robbery. A young ruffian knocked down an elderly man and stole several bars of silver that the man was carrying in his satchel. I rushed to give the victim aid, but the thief was long gone. I helped the man return to town, but there was nothing that could be done to restore his lost silver.

Some fifteen years later, I was passing through a distant town over Sukkos. As I entered the main *shul*, I noticed a man, who did not seem to be particularly religious, carrying a beautiful esrog box. The man's acquaintance admired the box and asked him where he had acquired it.

"I had it made," the man said carelessly. "I got hold of some silver bars, a long time ago. From an old man." He snickered.

As the man's words sank in, I looked at him more carefully. I could hardly believe it! It was the thief I had seen so many years ago, robbing the old man of his silver bars! I was shocked at the man's callousness. He assaulted an old man, robbed him, and then had the audacity to use that silver for an esrog box?!

I longed to have him charged and arrested, but I realized that I had no proof. Besides, the old man had died a long time before, and had no family to inherit his possessions. Reluctantly, I decided to let the matter drop.

I married some time later and settle in the same town. All went well for the first seven years after my marriage. Then a series of bloody pogroms swept the city. On one such occasion, I found myself hiding in an alleyway, directly opposite the store that belonged to the thief who had stolen those silver bars so many years before. As I hid there, I saw one of the peasants run out of the store, clutching the silver esrog box to his chest. When it was safe, I crept out of my hiding place and peeked into the store. The store owner had been savagely beaten, and he was unquestionably dead.

About ten years later, my business took me to a city some sixty or seventy miles away from my hometown. I was invited to stay at a certain person's home, and I was shocked to see the very same esrog box in his display cabinet!

"Where did you get that?" I asked.

"It's a strange story," the man replied. "Ten years ago, during the wave of pogroms, I hid in the fields to escape the peasants. When I went to the river to get a drink of water, I found a body there — a peasant who had drowned. He still clutched a satchel in his fist. I opened it carefully and discovered the esrog box. I realized that the man must have stolen it from another Jew. I didn't want an object that had been used for a *mitzvah* to be defiled, so I took it and fled." He looked at the box. "It is special, isn't it?"

"More special than you think," I replied dryly. I didn't tell him the story, though. I felt that if Hashem had placed that esrog box in his hands, that was where it belonged.

Several years after that incident, I returned to the same town to transact business again. My former host welcomed me back into his home. During my stay there, I realized that the esrog box was gone.

"What happened to the silver esrog box?" I asked.

The man looked rueful. "My son had a great deal of trouble with his business," he replied. "He lost so much money that he couldn't pay his taxes. The king's men came to the house and confiscated the esrog box as payment for my sons' debts."

I commiserated with him for his loss, but I couldn't help wondering where the esrog box would turn up next.

Reb Gershon listened spellbound to the story, but Reb Alter wasn't finished yet.

"The saga continues some five years later," Reb Alter continued. "The king was deposed and his successor had an advisor, a religious Jew, whom he greatly respected. The new ruler gave this Jew the esrog box as a gift."

"So how did it end up in our *shul*?" Reb Gershon asked.

"I remember the fellow," Reb Alter explained. "He lived right here in town. A very fine man, but unfortunately, he had no children. He bequeathed the esrog box to the *shul* when he died; that was about forty years ago."

The two men sat in silence, contemplating the incredible history that surrounded a single silver esrog box.

The Vilna Gaon interprets the passage of *Chad Gadya* as follows:

A kid that my father bought for two *zuzim* refers to the first born rights which were taken from Eisav and subsequently given to Yosef;

The cat refers to the other tribes — Yosef's brothers, who were jealous of Yosef's special coat — who acted jealous as a cat and sold Yosef because of the first born rights;

The dog that bit the cat refers to the Egyptians, whose enslavement of the Jews was caused by the sin of selling Yosef;

The stick that beat the dog refers to the staff of Moshe *Rabbeinu* that was used to redeem the Jews and smite Pharaoh and the Egyptians. The staff endured until the destruction of the holy *Beis Hamikdash*;

Then came fire that burnt the stick — this refers to the flame which destroyed the *Beis Hamikdash*, because of the sin of idol worship;

Then came water, and extinguished the fire — this refers to the men of the Great Assembly, who returned and rebuilt the Beis Hamikdash;

The ox who drank the water is Edom, who destroyed the second *Beis Hamikdash*;

The slaughterer that slaughtered the ox is *Mashiach ben Yosef*;

Then came the angel of death, and killed the slaughterer — this refers to Samel, who will kill *Mashiach ben Yosef*; and finally, came the Holy One, blessed is He, and slew the angel of death — Hashem Himself will bring *Mashiach ben David*.

Chad Gadya teaches us the importance of faith in Hashem's ultimate justice. He rewards those who do good and punishes those that commit evil. Situations may arise that we don't understand, events might unfold that defy our human comprehension, but the lesson of *Chad Gadya* teaches us that Hashem's providence guides everything that ever happens, in the past, the present and in the future!

····>━━•━━━•━━•<····

Laws
and
Customs

····>━━•━━━•━━•<····

*Laws and Customs**

EREV PESACH

1. From noon on Erev Pesach onward, one should only do the kind of work that is permitted on *Chol Hamoed*. However, repairing or cleaning clothes which one will wear for Yom Tov is permitted.
2. One should take a haircut or shave before midday, although one may have a non-Jew cut one's hair after midday.

THE FOUR CUPS OF WINE

3. At each *seder*, men, women and children are required to drink four full cups of wine. These must be drunk at the designated points in the *seder*, and one must recline while drinking them.
4. If possible, one should drink the entire cup of wine. If this is difficult, it is sufficient to drink the majority of the cup's contents or a *melo lugmav*, a mouthful, whichever is greater.
5. The cup itself must hold a *reviis*, even if one will not be able to drink more than a *melo lugmav*.
6. How much is a *reviis*? A *reviis* is the volume of one and a half eggs, estimated as being 170 cc./5.6 fl. oz. (the opinion quoted in the name of the Brisker Rav *lechumrah*), 150 cc./4.95 fl. oz. (the opinion of the Chazon Ish *lechumra*), 130 cc./4.42 fl. oz. (the opinion of Rav Moshe Feinstein *lechumrah*) 86 cc./2.9 fl. oz. (the opinion of the *Shiurei Tzion*). Although there are other *poskim* who estimate it as being as large as 230 cc., it is widely accepted to follow the estimate of 150 cc. for *d'Oraysa* biblical obligations and 86 cc. for most *d'Rabbanan* obligations. There-

---

* "Laws and Customs" section was compiled by Rabbi Avraham Marmorstein.

fore, one should certainly follow the stricter opinion for the first cup of wine when the *seder* is on a Friday night and according to most opinions, for the first cup of wine at the *seder* on any night of the week. It is desirable to follow the stricter opinion for all the four at the *seder*, unless someone will feel unwell as a result, or if there are medical reasons to drink a lesser quantity.

7. One should drink most of a *reviis* without stopping or with only a slight pause between gulps. At the very most, one must drink it within the time of *kedei achilas pras*, which we approximate for this purpose at two minutes. For the first two cups, one should be especially careful not to wait even two minutes but drink the full amount with only the shortest pauses. If one delayed in drinking the full amount, one should drink another cup. (A sick person who can only swallow with great difficulty may drink the wine within nine minutes).

8. Grape juice may be used for the four cups, but many *poskim* say that it should only be used by those who cannot tolerate wine or will be very uncomfortable or drowsy from wine. (A mixture of wine with a smaller part of grape juice would certainly be permitted.)

9. It is preferable to drink wine which has no sugar or other additives.

10. Some *poskim* say that it is preferable to use wine which has not been boiled (non-*mevushal*), but if as a result the wine may become forbidden by the contact of someone who renders it *stam yeinam*, one should certainly use *yayin mevushal*.

11. It is preferable to use red wine.

12. One may add water to wine in order to make it pleasant to drink, if that is the usual custom. However, if the winemaker has already added water to the wine (or grape juice), then one may only add a small amount of water, so that the proportion of wine should not be too low. (Ashkenazim generally require that the natural wine be at least one sixth, Sefarim require it to be the majority.)

13. The cups should be poured for each person by someone else, as a sign that this is a banquet of liberation.

14. One should not drink wine between the first and second cups or between the third and fourth, but one may drink wine between the second and third cups, i.e. during the meal. Water, seltzer or tea may be drunk between the first and second cup, and water may be drunk even between the third and fourth cup.

MATZAH

15. One should prepare before the *seder* enough *shemurah matzah* for each adult present to eat at least three, and preferably five, *kezeisim*. A *kezayis* is the volume of one olive.

16. Three whole *matzos* are placed on the *seder* table under a cover or in a tiered dish. According to the opinion of the *Vilna Gaon*, only two *matzos* are placed in the dish.

17. Some people make a particular effort to use *matzos* that were baked on the afternoon of *Erev Pesach*, since that is the time of the offering of the *Pesach* sacrifice. Most *poskim* agree that this is only a custom and not mandatory.

18. The *shemurah matzos* should be baked by a Jewish adult. When no one else can do it, they can be baked by non-Jews or children, but a Jewish adult must stand over them and remind them to bake for the purpose of the *mitzvah*.

19. Even sick people who may eat egg *matzos* (or any *matzos* made with fruit juice) on Pesach, cannot fulfill the *mitzvah* of eating *matzah* with them.

20. There are some opinions that permit the use of machine *matzos* baked with flour supervised carefully from the time the wheat was harvested, even for the *mitzvah* of eating *matzah* at the *seder*.

21. Most opinions say that the *matzos* of the *seder* should be hand made, even those who permit the use of machine *matzah* during the rest of Pesach. Some opinions actually prefer machine-made *matzah* throughout Pesach. And some forbid all machine-made *matzah* throughout Pesach.

22. For the initial *mitzvah* of eating *matzah,* one should eat one *kezayis* from the top *matzah* and one *kezayis* from the middle *matzah.*

23. How much is a *kezayis*? Much has been written in rabbinic literature attempting to define the exact size of the *kezayis* for all purposes. To summarize, some say that we can assume that the size of an average olive of today will automatically be adequate. Others say that the determining factor is the size of an olive in the time of the *Mishnah,* which may not be the same as today. Since many *poskim* expressed the opinion that olives are smaller now than they were in the time of the *Mishnah,* we are more stringent when it is relevant to a *d'Oraysa* obligation and define the *kezayis* as approximately double the size of today's olives. Thus, for the first *kezayis* of *matzah* one should follow the more stringent definition of a *kezayis,* unless health reasons or extreme discomfort prevent them from doing so. Therefore, a person should try to eat *matzah* of the volume of 50 cc./1.65 fl. oz. for the first *kezayis* and if possible, for the *afikoman.* For *korech* one may rely on the opinion the 33 cc./1.1 fl. oz. is sufficient. A sick person may rely on the opinion that 17 cc. .56 fl. oz. is sufficient.

24. The two *kezeisim* eaten for *motzi matzah* should be eaten together, ideally, inserted into the mouth at one time. If that is not easily possible, the *matzah* should be eaten within the time of *kedai achilas pras*-a time-span that we consider, for this purpose, to be approximately two minutes or according to a more lenient opinion, nine minutes. (Although there are also other opinions as to the duration of *kedai achilas pras,* one should try to follow the more stringent opinion since this is a *mitzvah d'Oraysa.*)

25. The *matzah* should be chewed until its flavor is discerned, not merely swallowed.

26. On the *seder* night, one does not dip the *matzah* in salt. Some have the custom to dip the *matzah* in salt, but then carefully shake the *matzah* to remove the salt.

27. Everyone at the table should receive enough *matzah* to eat two *kezeisim*.

28. Since eating *matzah* on the *seder* night is a *mitzvah d'Oraysa*, one should deliberately intend to fulfill the *mitzvah* at the moment that one eats the *matzah*. It is desirable that one should also think, at that moment, of the reason mentioned in the Torah for the eating of matzah on this night-that the dough did not have time to rise because Hashem so hastily redeemed our ancestors from Egypt.

29. The sick or elderly may eat crushed *matzah* for the *mitzvah*.

30. The *matzah* should be eaten without any other food or condiment, so that the flavor of the *matzah* not be mixed with other flavors.

KE'ARAH: THE SEDER PLATE

31. One should prepare a large plate, tray or specially made *ke'arah* which has spaces for the items that must be displayed on the *seder* table: the shankbone, the roasted egg, the *maror* (bitter herbs), the *charoses* and, according to most opinions, also the *karpas* (parsley).

32. According to the *Maharil* and the *Rema*, everything is placed on the *ke'arah* in the order it will be used. Whatever is used earlier is closer to the person leading the *seder*.

33. According to the *Vilna Gaon*, the shankbone and the egg should be placed closest to the person leading the *seder*, the two *matzos* (the *Vilna Gaon* did not use the third *matzah*) are placed in the middle, and *maror* and *charoses* are on the other side. (The *karpas* is not placed on the *ke'arah*, and the *ke'arah* is only brought to the table for *yachatz*, after eating the *karpas*.)

34. According to the *Arizal*, there are six items on the *ke'arah*, and they are arranged at the points of two triangles. According to the *Arizal* there should be two forms of bitter herbs on the *ke'arah*. The second one is reserved for *korech*. This is the most common way to arrange the *ke'arah*. (See diagram on following page)

The Ke'arah

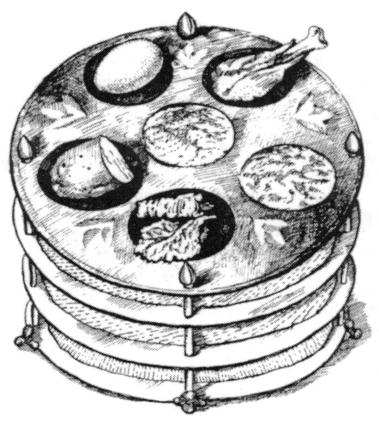

ביצה ROASTED EGG		זרוע SHANKBONE
	מרור MAROR	
כרפס VEGETABLE		חרוסת SWEET DIP
	חזרת HORSERADISH	

35. One should prepare the salt water, the *charoses*, the *zeroa* (shankbone) and the *beitzah* (roasted egg) before Yom Tov. If these were not prepared before Yom Tov, they can be prepared on the first night of Pesach, before the *seder*, but one should roast a bone and egg which will be eaten the next morning, since one may not cook food on Yom Tov unless it will be eaten that day.

36. When preparing the *charoses* at night before the *seder*, one should not grate the ingredients in the usual way. Instead, one should grate them with the reverse side of the grater or make another change in the method of grating.

37. When preparing salt water on Yom Tov, one should make a change in the usual method, for instance, by pouring the water in and then adding the salt.

KARPAS: THE FIRST DIP

38. After making *kiddush* and washing one's hands, one dips the *karpas* in salt water. For *karpas* one may use various vegetables. One can use any kind of vegetable over which the *berachah* of *Borei Pri Haadamah* is made but should not use fruit even if it is of a kind over which one makes *Borei Pri Haadamah.*

39. The word *karpas* has a special meaning, in addition to being the name of the type of vegetable to be used. It has the letters *perech samech*, hinting at the *avodas perech* — slave labor that the six hundred thousand Jewish people were forced to perform in Egypt. Therefore, many *gedolim* used only the vegetable called *karpas* in the time of the *Talmud*. This was identified by some as parsley, and by others as celery. (If one uses parsley very careful cleansing and inspection is necessary to ensure that it is not infested by insects.)

40. Some have the custom to use a boiled potato, either alone or together with a small amount of parsley, for *karpas*.

41. Some use radish for *karpas*. Others use an onion, although one should be careful not to take a bitter onion over which one could not say the *berachah* of *Borei Pri Haadamah.*

42. One should not use for *karpas* any of the varieties of vegetables which could be used for maror.

43. One should eat less than a *kezayis* for *karpas,* according to most poskim. The *Rambam* and some others are of the opinion that one should eat a *kezayis* of *karpas,* and it is recorded that the *Vilna Gaon* ate a *kezayis* of *karpas.* (The *Brisker Rav* and the *Chazon Ish* followed this opinion.)

44. Although one of the reasons for eating less than a *kezayis* is to avoid the question of whether or not to make the *berachah* of *Borei Nefashos,* if someone eats a *kezayis,* deliberately or by mistake, he or she does not say *Borei Nefashos.*

45. Holding the *karpas* in one's hand-not with a fork or spoon — one should dip it in the salt water and then make the *berachah* of *Borei Pri Haadamah* and eat the *karpas.* One should have in mind that the *berachah* should also be for the *Maror.*

46. Some permit the removal of the *karpas* and the saltwater from the table immediately. Others say that one should leave them on the table until after eating the *matzah* and *maror.*

MAROR: THE BITTER HERBS

47. Either one or two varieties of bitter herbs should be on the for the *mitzvah* of *maror.* Each person present must eat a *kezayis* of the *maror* and should eat an additional *kezayis* for *korech.* However, it is not necessary to use the *maror* that is on the *ke'arah.* One should estimate the *kezayis* of *maror* as 1.1 fl. oz. /33 cc., and for the purpose of korech one may estimate it as .56 fl. oz./17 cc.

48. The *Mishnah* gives the names of five species that may be used as *maror.* We can only identify two of them today. *Chazeres* (lettuce, which others identify specifically as romaine lettuce) and *tamcha* (horseradish).

49. Many *poskim* say that lettuce is the most desirable choice for *maror,* even if though it may be sweet and not particularly bitter. The lettuce must be thoroughly cleaned to ensure that

there are no insects in the leaves. For this reason, many people will only use the stalks of romaine lettuce and cut away the leaves.

50. If one uses horseradish for *maror,* most *poskim* agree that it should be ground or grated.

CHAROSES: THE SWEET DIP FOR MAROR

51. The *charoses* on the *seder* plate serves two purposes: It is commemorative of the mortar that was used in the slave labor of construction that the Jews were forced to do in Mitzrayim and of the apple tree which provided shade for the women who gave birth there, and it removes any possible danger that may be caused by the extreme bitterness of the *maror.*

52. The base for the *charoses* mixture should be one of the five fruits to which Israel is compared in *Shir Hashirim:* apples, pomegranates, dates, walnuts and almonds.

53. The *charoses* mixture should be of a thick texture but not very thick or very liquid.

KIDDUSH

54. Before *kiddush,* many people have the custom to recite the order of the *seder* as it is printed in the *Haggadah* — kadesh, urchatz, karpas, etc. — which is widely ascribed to *Rashi* or one of the *Baalei Tosafos.*

55. All the people at the *seder* table should have a *kiddush* cup before them since this is the first of the four cups of the *seder.*

56. Some say that even those who stand during *kiddush* on Friday night should sit during *kiddush* at the *seder.*

57. Others say that even at the *seder* one should recite *kiddush* while standing.

58. If a woman is making the *seder* alone or with other women only, and she recited Shehecheyanu when she lit the candles earlier, she does not repeat the *Shehecheyanu* in *kiddush.*

59. When Pesach begins on *motzei Shabbos, havdalah* is included in *kiddush* according to the order printed in the *haggadah* (*yaknehaz*). If one forgot to include *havdalah* in *kiddush* and remembered before eating *karpas*, one should immediately recite *havdalah* over another cup of wine.

60. If one did not realize the omission of *havdalah* until after eating *karpas*, one should wait until the end of *maggid* and the time of drinking the second cup of wine and insert the text of *havdalah*.

61. If one remembers the omission of *havdalah* during the eating of the meal, one should immediately recite *havdalah* and *borei meorei haesh* over a full cup of wine. However, one does not recite *borei pri hagafen*.

HESEIBAH: RECLINING

62. A person must recline on the left side while drinking all four cups of wine and eating *matzah, korech* and the *afikoman*. (Although there are some opinions that exempt an *aveil* within the year of mourning for his parents or who has just completed *shivah* for another immediate family member from reclining altogether, this is not the general custom.)

63. It is desirable for a person to eat the entire meal while reclining. Some say that it is mandatory to try to recline throughout the meal. One is not required to recline during the recitation of *maggid* and not during the eating of *maror*.

64. Some say that one should recline during the eating of *karpas*.

65. Most *poskim* exempt women from reclining. However, they may recline if they wish, and it is praiseworthy to do so. The custom among Sefardim is for women to recline.

MAGGID: TELLING THE EXODUS STORY

66. One should have in mind or say aloud that one is about to fulfill the *mitzvah d'Oraysa* of telling the story of the Exodus from Egypt.

67. The *matzah, maror* and all of the other customary foods should be on the table and visible to all when the story of the exodus from Egypt is being told.

68. The story of the Exodus from Egypt should be told in the form of questions and answers. The normal way to do this is to have a child ask the questions of the *mah nishtanah*. Some people encourage all the children present to ask the questions. If only one child asks the *mah nishtanah*, it should be a child who understands the questions, not a child so young as the memorize them without comprehension. Even if there is no child present, the adults should ask each other the *mah nishtanah.*

69. The words of the *haggadah* should be recited aloud and they should be translated or explained in the language understood by all present if they do not understand the Hebrew text. If those listening cannot have the entire *haggadah* translated for them, they should at least hear *mah nishtanah, avadim hayinu,* the listing of the ten plagues and the explanations of *pesach, matzah* and *maror* translated or explained. (These are vital for the minimum fulfillment of the *mitzvah* of telling the story of *Yetzias Mitzrayim.*) If this is impossible, the translation in a printed *haggadah* should be read by those present who do not understand Hebrew, reading the translation of each paragraph as it is being recited.

70. The *haggadah* should be recited with respect and seriousness and, at the same time, in a joyous manner. One should not interrupt the recital of the *haggadah* except to discuss and explain the story of *Yetzias Mitzrayim* or other relevant matters.

71. According to many opinions, the discussion of the laws of Pesach is also part of the *mitzvah* of telling about the exodus from Egypt.

72. The custom is for the head of the household to read and explain the *haggadah* aloud, but it is preferable for each person to read along quietly.

INSUFFICIENT TIME

73. If there is not enough time for the entire *haggadah*, one should recite *kiddush*, *ha lachma anya*, *mah nishtanah*, *avadim hayinu*, *mitchilah ovdei avodah zara*, *Rabban Gamliel haya omer* and *asher g'alanu*, eat *matzah*, *maror*, *korech* and *afikoman* and drink the first two *kosos* at the appropriate points.

74. If someone has only a few minutes and cannot even recite all of this before midnight, he or she should give a priority to *Rabban Gamliel hayah omer* and then eat *matzah* and *maror*. Other *poskim* say that the greatest priority should be given to *avadim hayinu* or a summary of *Yetzias Mitzrayim*. If there is no time for this, one should make *kiddush*, drink the first cup of wine, wash one's hand and eat a *kezayis* of *matzah*, eat a *kezayis* of *maror* before midnight and then say the whole *haggadah* and eat the meal.

THE AFIKOMAN

75. The *afikoman*, the larger part of the broken *matzah*, is eaten after the meal before *birchas hamazon*.

76. One must eat at least a *kezayis* of the *afikoman* within the time limit of *kdei achilas pras* (2 or 9 minutes, as explained).

77. According to some opinions, the *kezayis* of the *afikoman* is the main eating of *matzah* of the evening. Therefore, one should be very careful to eat an adequate quantity and to have in mind to fulfill the *mitzvah d'Oraysa* of *matzah*.

78. It is preferable to eat two *kezeisim* of the *afikoman*, one to commemorate the *korban pesach* and one for the *matzah* that was eaten with it.

79. If one cannot find the piece of the middle *matzah* designated as *afikoman*, any other *matzah* may be substituted.

80. The *afikoman* should be eaten by *chatzos*.

81. If one cannot finish the meal by *chatzos*, there are many *poskim* who permit one to eat the *afikoman* earlier in the meal before

midnight with a verbal stipulation that if the *halachah* requires the *afikoman* to be eaten before midnight, this shall be considered the *afikoman*, and if this is not required then this is merely *matzah* eaten as part of the meal. Then one waits until midnight, eats the rest of the meal and eats another *afikoman*, with the stipulation that if the earlier one was *afikoman* then this is not.

82. After eating the *afikoman*, one may not eat anything else until the next morning. If one accidentally ate some other food after the *afikoman* and has not yet *bentched*, one should eat another *kezayis* of *matzah*. One may not drink any wine after the remaining two *kosos* but may drink water, tea or coffee. Some permit other juices or beverages.

83. If one forgot to eat the *afikoman* and started to say *birchas hamazon* one should complete *birchas hamazon* and wash again in order to eat the *afikoman*. This would also apply if one remembered after the end of *birchas hamazon* but before saying *borei pri hagafen* over the third cup.

84. If one had already drunk the third cup of wine, some *poskim* say that one should not wash again to eat the forgotten *afikoman* but should consider the *matzah* eaten during the meal as sufficient to fulfill the *mitzvah*.

85. However, one who sometimes recites *birchas hamazon* without a cup of wine throughout the year should wash again and eat the *afikoman*, followed by *birchas hamazon* without a cup of wine, no matter how late in the *haggadah* one remembers, even after concluding the entire *seder*.

86. If one forgot the *afikoman* and had not eaten a *kezayis* of *matzah* within a *kedei achilas pras* during the meal, all *poskim* agree that one should wash again and eat another *kezayis*.

87. If one was a guest at the *seder* where an inadequate amount of *matzah* was provided for each guest to fulfill the *mitzvah* and returns home before midnight, one should wash again at home and eat a *kezayis* of *shemurah matzah* without repeating the *berachah* of *al achilas matzah*.

88. If one returned home after midnight and had definitely not eaten a *kezayis* of *shemurah matzah* at any point during the *seder* or had eaten a *kezayis* of *matzah* at the beginning of the meal but had not had a *kezayis* for the *afikoman*, one should wash and eat a *kezayis* of *shemurah matzah*. If it is after midnight and one is not sure if the amount of *matzah* served was sufficient, a *rav* should be consulted since the *halachah* would depend on the exact circumstances.

89. Even after eating the *afikoman*, one should leave over some *matzah* on the *seder* table until the end of the entire *haggadah*.

HALLEL AND THE SEDER CONCLUSION

90. Before reciting *Hallel*, the cups of all present should be refilled, in order that *Hallel* be recited over a cup of wine.

91. Although it is not mandatory, the custom is for the leader of the *seder* to pour a fifth cup, which is called *kos shel Eliyahu*, the cup of Elijah.

92. Some say that one should try to complete the recitation of *Hallel* before midnight.

93. Although the *Haggadah* is recited by the leader while the others listen or say it quietly, *Hallel* should be recited aloud by everyone.

94. Although the rest of *Hallel* is recited by everyone together, *hodu* in *Hallel* should be recited by the leader and the others should respond *hodu*. Similarly, for *yomar na* and *yomru na*, the leader should recite it and the others respond.

95. For this purpose, one should try to have at least two people present in addition to the leader of the *seder*. One may count women (or, if necessary, children who are old enough to understand) for this purpose, since women are also obligated to recite the *Hallel* on the *seder* night.

96. At the end of *Hallel* the recitation of *ana Hashem* is also done in this responsive manner. However, one can ask a child to lead in the saying of *ana Hashem* but not in the saying of *hodu*.

97. Some *poskim* are of the opinion that on the *seder* night one must understand *Hallel* in order to fulfill the *mitzvah*. To fulfill the *mitzvah* of *Hallel* according to all opinions, someone who does not understand Hebrew should follow the text in a translation.

98. Even an *aveil*, a mourner, who as not yet observed *shivah* before *Yom Tov*, recites *Hallel* at the *seder*.

99. The *zemiros* at the end of the *haggadah* — *vayehi bachatzi halayla, veamartem zevach pesach, ki lo naeh, adir hu, echad mi yodeia* and *chad gadya* — are not an integral part of the *seder*, but it is a widespread custom to sing them after *nirtzah*. Many *poskim* emphasized that they must be treated with great respect.

100. After the *seder*, one may drink water, tea or coffee (or seltzer) but not other foods or drinks, or order that the taste of the *afikoman* should remain in one's mouth all night. To drink other drinks is permitted only if there is a special need.

THE SECOND SEDER

101. Outside Eretz Yisrael, two days of Yom Tov are observed, and a *seder* must be made the second night with all the care and stringency of the first night's *Seder*.

102. Those who eat an especially large quantity of *matzah* for the first *kezayis* because it is *mitzvah d'Oraysa*, may be more lenient the second night and eat the same quantity as for the later *kezayis*.

103. The generally accepted practice is to count *sefiras haomer* on the second night at the end of *Maariv* and before the commencement of the second *seder*.

104. Some prefer to recite *sefiras haomer* at the end of the *seder*.

WHEN EREV PESACH IS A SHABBOS

105. When *erev* Pesach is a *Shabbos*, those who normally are particular to eat *matzos* baked on *erev* Pesach bake them instead on

Friday afternoon. Some are particular to bake the *matzos* after Shabbos immediately before the *Seder*.

106. Some *poskim* are the opinion that on the Friday afternoon before Shabbos *erev* Pesach one should not do work after midday, as if it was *erev* Yom Tov.

107. One may prepare the salt water, *charoses*, the *zeroa* (shankbone) and the *beitzah* (roasted) egg before Shabbos. If these were not prepared before Shabbos, they cannot be prepared on Shabbos. When preparing on *motzaei* Shabbos, the first night of Pesach, one should roast a bone and egg which will be eaten the next morning, since one may no cook food of Yom Tov unless it will be eaten that day.

108. When preparing *charoses* on *motzaei* Shabbos, one should not grate apples or other ingredients in the usual way. Instead one should grate with the reverse side of the grater, or make another change in the methods of grating.

109. When preparing salt water on *motzaei* Shabbos, one should make a change in the usual method, for instance, by pouring the water in and then adding salt.